Light on a Hill

Dedication

*I dedicate this book
in precious remembrance of
all the faithful members of the Whitewell Fellowship
past and present,
also to my
very dear friends
John and Dale
Estlinbaum,
Friendswood, Texas
whose love has been
supportive these many years*

Light on a Hill:

The Story of the Whitewell Church

James McConnell

Marshall Pickering

Marshall Morgan and Scott
Marshall Pickering
3 Beggarwood Lane, Basingstoke, Hants RG23 7LP, UK

British Library Cataloguing in Publication Data

McConnell, James
　　Light on a hill: the story of the
　　Whitewell Church.
　　1. Spiritual life
　　I. Title
　　269　　　　BV4501.2

　　ISBN 0–7208–0700–X

Text set in Linotron Century by
Input Typesetting Ltd, London SW19 8DR
Printed in Great Britain by
Richard Clay Ltd, Bungay, Suffolk

Contents

Foreword

The names Whitewell and Jim McConnell are synony-
mous. The Whitewell story is about the Pastor and
place that have seen thousands of souls won for Jesus
Christ. It is written by the man who knows it best, he
was part of those humble beginnings with ten people
thirty years ago.

The pages reveal the struggles, the disappointments
and the sacrifices faced by those involved in this ever
growing church. It is, however, the account of how a
people who love the Lord are more than conquerors in
what often looked like insurmountable obstacles.
When a target set by the Pastor seemed to be beyond
reach, they climbed that mountain and always had
energy and faith left to climb further. The 'second-
mile' to them is normal motorway.

This timely contribution of great exploits for God
can do nothing but excite and encourage Christians to
see Him move in their lives. Appetites will be whetted
with a hunger for God as the discerning reader looks
for seed sown to produce a harvest. The same type of
harvest that Jim McConnell has come to live with.
His plans have been no passing whim, whether the
erection of a beautiful sanctuary or filling the Kings
Hall, dreams become realities, hopes materialize. In
this church a born leader leads his troops from one

venture of faith to another. He knows his army and is always aware of the enemy.

The story is not about 'shots in the dark'. Prayer, hearing from God, the prophetic word, are integral parts of thirty years on the Whitewell road. Expository preaching is no small reason for the faith of the 'Whitewellers' as their Pastor affectionately calls them.

Adversity and trials are met by a deep rooted faith in the word of God. The shepherd's continuous study of the book of books has given birth to a big church with big people.

Chapters vibrate with the writer's passion for souls, the evangelist's heart-throb can be heard, as the pages unfold. His desire to reach the lost as a fourteen-year-old boy in East Belfast has not diminished but rather intensified with the passing of years. Areas of his life may have mellowed through grace and maturity but the tramp of the lost on the way to Hell and eternal punishment move him as few preachers in Ulster are moved today.

The book vividly describes how the boy preacher becomes a man in God; it is heart touching, so written that faith and confidence in the promises of God will become the blessing of every reader.

I feel honoured to be asked to introduce this book; of recent years the author has become a beloved friend and a loyal companion, as we work as fellow labourers in the Gospel. I pray through this publication of how God can move in one church that the fires of revival will ignite in all our churches so that in this beloved province sinners will be converted and His name glorified.

Eric McComb
President of the Elim Pentecostal Church
1987–88

Introduction

It was a dismal Sunday night in January – the 25th, in fact. There was a cold icy wind, and the rain coming down did not help matters as I walked, under a borrowed umbrella, from my home to the Whitewell Church which was approximately 200 yards away.

The time was 6.15 p.m. – the service would begin at 6.45 p.m. Usually in that short walk I cover myself by faith in the precious Blood of the Lord Jesus and once again ask God in His mercy to anoint me by the power of His gracious Holy Spirit. There would not be much time to pray as I entered the foyer of the church. Always, someone is waiting to see me – a distressed mother, a single-parent father seeking advice, or an enthusiastic youth anxious to hear my views on some text he has just read.

My excitement soared because I had decided to preach on the subject, 'Abortion – the Licensed Murder of Babies'. But with the excitement, I was a trifle nervous as such subjects are not my usual forte: I stole the title for my sermon from a book written by a Lutheran Minister's wife whose child unwittingly saw an abortion on television, and cried out with alarm: 'Who broke the baby?'

As I turned the corner I wondered if many people would be there. The road was jammed with cars, the side streets packed bumper to bumper. At the church car park, there were my deacons standing in the rain trying to direct and accommodate everyone as the 45-seater buses queued in a long line in order to let their passengers disembark.

At twenty minutes to seven Irwin Rea led the Song Service. As I mounted the high pulpit, I could see every aisle was blocked with extra chairs. The back doors were pushed open – people were sitting in the hallway, children were sitting around the pulpit area, to make room for adults. Suddenly, I was aware that behind me the curtains were being opened as hurriedly chairs were placed into the very baptistry to seat people. Two packed nurseries were in operation at the same time. 1,600 people had crowded in to hear what the Holy Spirit had to say about abortion!

As I sat in the pulpit my mind wandered back to the first time I had ministered on the Whitewell Road. In fact by the next month, February, I would be thirty years in the pastorate of this church.

What a flood of memories came back as I watched the reaction on the faces of the people as that great congregation worshipped God: ex-terrorists, bombers, gunmen, con-men, alcoholics, drug addicts, prostitutes, policemen, prison warders, court clerks, Protestants and Catholics from both sides of the religious and political divide – all changed by the power of God. Unified in Christ! Born again! Rejoicing in God's sovereign grace! What a mixed bunch. I was reminded of the visit of Bernard Falk from the BBC to Whitewell to find out what was going on. He said he felt Whitewell was a refuge for terrorists. However, I replied that Whitewell was like a modern Cave of Adullam – that cave where we are told all that were in debt, all that were in distress, all that were discontented, gathered themselves unto David and he became a captain over them! Only this time the captain in Whitewell was none other than David's greater son – the Lord Jesus Christ! All this was a far cry from February 23rd 1957 when ten people met to break bread and remember the Lord's death in a rented, cold, Orange Hall, sitting under a small heater!

The total offerings that day amounted to £8.7s.10d., barely enough to meet the expenses of the rent, heat, light and advertising! Today the grand total of the offerings would amount to just over £8,000, to meet the commitments of our foreign missionaries, our Home Missions Department and of course our own Mother Church with her many facets of ministry.

Yes, indeed, the Whitewell story is a story of how Almighty God took an insignificant people with its young pastor and made them a household word throughout the Evangelical world!

If this story can inspire and encourage some struggling pastor or some discouraged local church then it is worth the telling and worth the writing.

But before I go any further I must say: to the Lord Jesus Christ, the Head of the Church, be all the glory!

1

Childhood

Life began for me in East Belfast, under the shadow of the great shipyard, Harland and Wolff, which in its heyday employed over 20,000 men.

My father, Edward McConnell, was known in those shipyard days as a 'driller'. It was in East Belfast that he met my mother – then Jean Anderson. They married and set up home in a little kitchen house at 14 Spring Street. The first child born into the McConnell family was my sister Lila, and seven years later I arrived on 15th May 1937.

Recollections of those early years are quite vivid because those were the days of the Second World War. I remember hearing the sirens (which, incidentally, each time made me cry), then overhead the noise of the bomber aeroplanes, and seeing the distant flare of the incendiary bombs as they were dropped to give light to the *Luftwaffe*.

Some nights my sister and I would be lifted from our bed by my parents and taken to an air-raid shelter down the street where the local residents would have a sing-song. Other times when a larger scale attack was feared we were again carried (on my father's shoulders) or taken in a pram to the Castlereagh Hills. When the 'all clear' siren sounded, we knew it was safe to return.

During the close of the War, on 19th June 1945, my

mother died. I was seven years and eleven months, my sister Lila was fourteen. The next five years were to be very traumatic years for me. Then, as a boy, I could not understand, but now as a man I can see that Almighty God in His lovely and sovereign grace was working out His purpose for my life!

Little did I know that in less than two years my father would be taken very ill with tuberculosis. My sister Lila, who was a beautiful girl, also contracted the disease which reduced her in weight to approximately 56lb. (4 stone). The shock waves that went through that little house at Spring Street were powerful for soon it was to be locked up for six years and I would have to live with my grandparents – the Andersons.

But something very significant happened some months before all this was to take place: I was attending the Iron Hall Sunday School where my grandfather, Joseph Anderson, was an elder. Week by week, I sat under the faithful, caring ministry of my Sunday School teacher, Sammy Jamison. He was the first person to tell me about God's plan of salvation and of how Jesus Christ loved me. Eventually he began to get through to me, as one Sunday afternoon I asked him if he would help me to come to the Lord Jesus.

I will never forget that day as he and I knelt down together at that old wooden bench where I asked the Lord Jesus to come into my heart. The Holy Spirit in His purpose was preparing my heart for the particular year that would lie ahead and indeed for the years that would follow.

One thing stands out during that first year of my conversion. I remember at Christmas receiving a book as a Sunday School prize: it was the story of William Carey, the cobbler God sent to India. His courage inspired me, particularly his courage when as a boy he fell from a tree, breaking his leg. His first ambition when able to walk once more was to go back to that same tree and climb it again! That's the sort of courage and determination I needed!

As a boy, my insecurity and uncertainty were alarming! I was beset by all sorts of fears. You may laugh – but there was an 'entry' leading from Cherryville Street to the old field at Spring Street where a water tank was situated and I had to walk down there to get home. The blackness of the night always unnerved me. I walked down that entry with two half bricks in my hand, whistling in the dark to comfort myself and to let any imaginary assailants know I wasn't afraid of them!

Looking back at my childish conduct then and comparing it with my behaviour now at fifty years of age, I still sometimes find when nervous or anxious over some great decision I have to make 'whistling in the dark'! Surely all adults have done the same thing at one time or another!

But to come back to that old book on William Carey: I remember distinctly getting out of bed and asking God if He thought I could do something for Him, would He take me and use me.

The front room of Spring Street was lit by a gas mantle – electricity was just beginning to be put into small homes. But as I turned to go back to bed that old gas mantle became larger and larger – until it seemed the whole room was like a magnified and glorified gas mantle! The presence and power of that light was tremendous. But the vision and the message of that presence gave me the assurance that the Lord Jesus was with me, and from that night I received the confidence I needed to face the problems and responsibilities of life. I believe what happened that night was a manifestation of the presence of the Holy Spirit making the Lord Jesus real to me. I am sure that some readers may conclude that either I was hallucinating or it was my imagination. I am convinced it was a

fulfilment of the prophecy given by the prophet Joel
in chapter 2, v. 28:

> In the last days, saith God, I will pour out my spirit
> upon all flesh; and your sons and your daughters
> shall prophesy, your old men shall dream dreams,
> your young men shall see visions: and also upon the
> servants and upon the handmaids in those days will
> I pour out my spirit.

All I know is from that night I obtained a strength
and a courage I had never known before. But little did
I know that experience would come back to me at
different intervals of my life, right up to the year 1973
when God mightly and graciously began to move in
the Whitewell Church.

But to get back to my childhood – the next four
years, separated from my father and sister, were very
difficult, but that sustaining presence helped me yet
again!

As I stated earlier, my sister began to grow much
weaker and as deterioration set in the doctors gave
her a limited time to live. But my Godly grandfather
lay on the hospital floor all night crying unto God for
her and God in His grace spared her life and put flesh
back on her bones! More and more I was discovering
the power of prayer and the desire to pray! Then on
28th November 1951, after being in hospital for four
years, my father died of cancer.

I really felt forsaken and alone!

What was going to happen to me? I was nearly fourteen years of age and needed direction. What was I
going to do with my life? Who could help me? Who
could advise me? What I write now will remain with
me all the days of my life!

After my father's funeral I was walking along the
Ravenhill Road to Park Parade School, where I was
educated. With tears running down my face, I began
to call upon God, then I began to sing:

Face with face with Christ my Saviour,
Face to face what will it be?
When with rapture I behold Him,
Jesus Christ who died for me.

That road – its activities, its noise, its bustle – faded away as I seemed to be guided by radar toward the school. Suddenly I heard myself singing in a language I had never known, never heard before and didn't even understand! My heart was pounding and beating as powerful utterances poured forth from my being like lava from a volcano. What was happening to me? What the Lord Jesus said in John 7:37–8: 'In the last day, that great day of the feast, Jesus stood and cried, saying, If any man thirst, let him come unto me, and drink. He that believeth on me, as the scripture hath said, out of his belly shall flow rivers of living water.'

I finally made my way to class where the first lesson was music. Our music teacher was a very talented young Welsh girl (the boys loved her). Usually at the end of the music lesson she would play a piece from the classic composers. But this day she decided to end the lesson with the hymn 'Abide with me'. As the boys sang we came to the verse:

Hold thou thy cross before my closing eyes,
Shine through the gloom and point me to the skies.

Can you imagine how I felt? Here I found myself worshipping God again after being saturated by His Spirit on the Ravenhill Road. It was too much for me – my eyes belched tears, my face was drenched in them. As I was wiping my tears with my jersey that mighty presence flowed through me again, like a torrent. I slumped on to the desk. My chum whom I played football with (and how we took the game seriously) asked, 'Are you ill? What's wrong with you?' I replied, 'I feel great.' He looked at me in sheer amazement!

Once again the Holy Spirit was manifesting Himself to me, reassuring me and empowering me for future days.

I would never be the same again!

Strange leadings

Soon after this I was led into a small Pentecostal
Church situated on My Ladys Road where I worked in
the Sunday School, testified in the open-air meetings
and gave a little word or two!

In fact, I preached my first sermon on a Sunday
morning from Psalm 22. My subject: 'The Sufferings
of Christ'. I was fourteen years of age.

That little church has now ceased and the majority
of its members have gone home to glory. At strength
there were about forty-five members and I will never
forget their love and kindness to me. It seemed I was
the only young person who was a member and
knowing I had no parents they utterly spoiled me,
making sure I wanted for nothing! I thank God for
every remembrance of them.

One couple who stood out among these precious
people were Billy Towell and his wife Lily. (He was
the man in those early years who started the Gospel
Meetings in the shipyard, giving every apprentice a
free gift of the New Testament.) This couple brought
me to their home many times where they taught me
how to conduct myself and how to have manners. What
a blessing they were!

As I look back over the years, I see how God sends
special people along life's way for the educating and
preparation of those whom He has a mind to use.

There are people whose touch can uplift and there are others whose influence can discourage. But that's the way we discover those who truly love us! Many times in my preaching I emphasise how each of us must become an influence for good. There are men whose touch only brings decay and corruption, but then there are others who bring you nothing but good! I have now been over thirty-three years in full-time ministry and can testify to both. As Paul beautifully penned in Romans 8:28: 'And we know that all things work together for good to them that love God, to them who are the called according to His purpose.' God in His gentleness was moulding me – He gave me a hunger to pray and read His word. It was incredible; every morning I would waken at 6.30 a.m. (no matter how late I went to bed) without an alarm clock to seek the face of the Lord.

I remember distinctly asking God to help me to understand and know His word. What I asked may encourage some 'vessel' He has called to work for Him to do the same. I had read what the Lord Jesus had said about the Holy Spirit in John 14:26: 'But the Comforter, which is the Holy Ghost, whom the Father will send in my name, He shall teach you all things, and bring all things to your remembrance, whatsoever I have said unto you.'

So I prayed: 'Lord, help me to absorb everything I read in your word, make my mind like a sponge, like a blotting paper that I will be able to retain and store it.' I used to 'colour' verses (in an old Schofield Bible) that impressed and inspired me until that old Bible was a mass of coloured markings! And even to this day, thirty-six years later, when I'm preaching – be it the Whitewell pulpit, other pulpits, or somewhere overseas – I can still see in my mind that old colour-marked Bible and I can still quote accurately from that old book!

My hunger for God's word intensified and I made it

my business to find out what books I should read.
Every day I read a Chapter and Exposition by
Matthew Henry, then after that a Sermon by Charles
Haddon Spurgeon, and to round it off a Character
Study by old Alexander Whyte. (Over recent years,
incidentally, I have gone back to this habit.) That's
what I cut my spiritual eye-teeth on and it gave me
the inside lining I needed to be strong and grasp God's
Word.

If there's a young pastor reading this – try it for
yourself! It will give a finesse and a depth to your
ministry and take away the shallowness that is very
evident in many pulpits today.

But God does not bless you all at once, neither does
He tell you all at once. He will lead you step by step
– there are no short cuts to His success, He takes you
by the long road. As it says in Exodus 13:17–18: 'And
it came to pass, when Pharaoh had let the people go,
that God led them not through the way of the land of
the Philistines, although that was near.' Five days
hard marching would have brought them to Canaan,
but the short cut was not God's way. Verse 18 says:
'But God led the people about, through the way of the
wilderness.' And this is what was going to happen to
me; but not only me, every other Servant of God He
has ordained for His purpose.

Led again

As the days and months went by, slowly but surely my capacity for prayer and the reading of God's word enlarged, until I realised God was about to bring me into another phase of His purpose. I was now fifteen years of age, and one morning whilst in intense prayer, the Holy Spirit told me to go to another group in the city who were not popular. My reaction to that leading was one of stubbornness and hesitancy. I shared this with some older Christians and they were alarmed at where I was to go! One dear old lady came to me with a dream she had had. She saw me drowning in a river where no friends were near at hand to help me. 'Don't go', she said. At that very same time a prominent Servant of God I idolised as a boy expressed a keen desire to take and train me for the ministry, and with all these strange things happening at once, I was thrown into a state of confusion. I found myself listening to too many people. So, for a while, I stifled and shelved that special leading I had in prayer.

But, during the next six months, I was to be taught a bitter lesson, even as a boy. If you disobey the Holy Spirit, God will let you know, and if you are a praying man or woman, you will be the first to know!

Every step of obedience you take, God will bless you for it; every backward step taken only brings you barrenness and dryness.

I eventually became aware that I wasn't touching
God the way I used to; or, rather, the truth was God
wasn't touching me the way He used to. Gone was that
sharpness, that keenness, that discernment to seize a
chance, an opportunity. I was sluggish, slow and actually struggling to pray. Some mornings I overslept. I
remember going to the drawing office (the 'design
squad') where I worked, first as a message boy then
later as a secretary, and rushing in to punch the clock.
Even the office staff noticed my lateness! Usually I
was in one hour before starting time because I had
been up at prayer. I would walk to work praying
constantly with each step I would take to the office.

What was wrong with me? It became obvious a
showdown between God and me had to come. It came!
One morning I used the lift to go to the Admiralty
office. Stopping the lift in mid-air (even though I was
always nervous of lifts) I cried: 'Father, what have I
done? I need you.' Suddenly that still small voice came,
saying: 'You have done nothing!' I knew immediately
what the Spirit was saying. I cried: 'But Lord, nobody
likes these people – they are heretics.' But the Spirit
said: 'Go!'

That morning, in the lift, I surrendered my whole
life to the Master. I would go, no matter what the
consequences. When the lift finally reached its desti-
nation, I walked out to find curious stares fastened
upon me. What was I doing or what had I been up to?

As I look back on it all, I ask, What if I hadn't
obeyed? There would not eventually have been a
Whitewell – or perhaps God would have chosen
someone else. But I went where God led me! Then a
very strange thing happened immediately after this:
I was sitting at my desk one morning when a young
man came in. He said 'Good morning', placed a note
in my hand then quickly walked away! I noted the
date – 5th November 1953. This is what was written:

The Lord showed a large store, and a man going into the store with lots of vessels; some were big, others were medium and the remainder were small. The man then filled each of the vessels to capacity with oil.

This typifies the Lord going into His storehouse and filling channels with the Message of Deliverance. Then the Lord looked on the great and mighty ones; they couldn't have the message because they were not willing to humble themselves and wait before Him in the secret place. Therefore He took the weak of the world and raised them with great power.

Then He looked on me. He saw that I was weak in mine own eyes but willing to humble myself before Him. He saw in my heart the desire to serve Him and because of this He would use me as one of those vessels.

But what sort of vessel would I like to be?

If I would be faithful in the capacity He would give me, He would enlarge that capacity and fill it with Himself. But in the meantime I must do what I had been commanded to do.

That was some message on a November morning! And it was – to me! The bearer of the message left me without a word. It shook me to my very foundation. God was in my life in the power of the Holy Spirit.

Once again as time progressed God brought two men into my life. In Northern Ireland they were always looked upon as controversial and heretical – but that was a matter of opinion. These two men had the ability and foresight to see the grace of God in my life and they gave me precious encouragement to pursue my ministry. There are some people in Ulster and in the United Kingdom who profess to have 'the truth' – but their attitudes and their lives are a contradiction to that which they preach. I can only say what I saw and what I found.

Pastors James Forsythe and Gordon Magee were Godly men – men of zeal and men with big hearts. Above all, men who were in love with Jesus Christ. They knew I was alone with a sister ill in hospital and both their homes were opened to me for love, comfort and teaching.

What did they teach me? James Forsythe taught me how to pray and worship and of the practical side of God's work. Gordon Magee – a master in the craft of preaching – taught me how to communicate and put across the message of God's grace for sinners and how to be constructive in my sermon preparation.

Again, I thank God for these men, for their love and kindness to me over those early and formative years. Both men have now retired but they will never be forgotten by me.

4

Whitewell

By this time I was preaching approximately three times a week. God in His grace was blessing His word with men and women coming to Christ.

On many occasions I was invited to England to speak at conventions and youth rallies. But my preaching engagements were beginning to interfere with my work in the drawing office. My bosses (unsaved men) were very kind to me, and at times when I was away covered for me, but I knew in my heart that this could not continue much longer.

All I thought about was praying, studying, witnessing and preaching, until at the 1955 Easter Convention on the 11th April a group of ministers from all over the world laid hands on me and ordained me to be an evangelist – thirty-four days before my eighteenth birthday!

One might say here, surely I was too young to fulfil such a task; and, humanly speaking, one would be right! The only thing I can say in my defence is, I became a burden to no one – financially or materially, living on meagre resources for many years. I believe it was God testing and pruning me to see what I wanted to serve him for.

What was my true motive? In the year I was ordained, over 500 people came to Christ. I was eighteen years of age!

Then in the month of August I was invited to the
North of England to do 'pulpit supply' for a minister
who was on an extended trip to the United States. In
retrospect, this again was a further preparation period
for the real work God had for me to do.

I recollect so vividly landing in Newcastle-upon-
Tyne, going on to Gateshead, and arriving at Dean
Street, there to be looked after by a precious little
widow. She had left a key for me to let myself in as
the house was empty. And the eighteen-year-old boy
with two cases in his hands, ready to turn the world
upside down and rightside up for God, wept with sheer
loneliness!

Now the man who had asked me to do pulpit supply
while he was visiting the USA told me I would personally receive a salary of £7.10s per week ... not bad
for those days of 1955! But I never saw it. The church
gave me 15s. each week, when they remembered, and
at times even forgot to pay my dear little widow the
£3 she was entitled to for looking after me! So there
were days of scarcity in Dean Street.

One day, the cupboard was really bare! My dear and
kind host suddenly remembered that she had some
empty lemonade bottles to be returned. She ran to the
shop and with what she got for the empties, was able
to purchase food for us to eat.

I was young, but mature enough to know that this
was a test of my love, my faith and my dedication to
the Lord Jesus to see how I would cope! But I tramped
the streets of Newcastle and Gateshead, visiting and
testifying – trying in my youth to prepare 'Holy Ghost'
intelligent and inspiring messages.

Many times as I recall those experiences, I think of
how God had told Elijah that at Zarephath He had
commanded a widow woman to sustain him while God
was preparing him for the work he had for him to do.
('Zarephath' means 'Smelting' – a place where metals
are refined.) That dear lady, Mrs Carr, whether she

realised it or not, was in the purpose of God to sustain me and look after me during those months.

As the days passed, our next door neighbours came to the Lord and in fact to the church. Their name happened to be the same as the little widow who looked after me. Mr Carr was a coal miner and took a kind and fatherly interest in me. Before long, those two families spoiled me with many kindnesses and acts of love. Just as God had ravens and a widow for Elijah so God had these lovely precious people for me. And when the time was come for me to return home to Ireland, they begged me to stay! I can tell you it was a sad day leaving them.

Once again, I thank God for every remembrance of them!

In the meantime, that small church at Gateshead was packed to capacity. More seats were installed and at times we had to rent a larger auditorium to house the crowds who were coming to hear the gospel. During these four months, without fail, every week men and women were coming to Christ. Big Geordie coal miners, rough and tough, but a fantastic bunch of men. Drunkards, alcoholics and even prostitutes were coming in and the Spirit of God was changing them and sanctifying them.

One night will live with me as long as I live – it was October 1955. I had been walking the roads of Gateshead and Newcastle praying and crying unto God that He might manifest His power and presence in a mighty way – strange things were happening to me!

I was waking in the middle of the night, weeping before the Lord – crying for Him that He would move by the power of His spirit.

Then one Sunday night, just before the service, my workers and I were having a time of prayer. The song service had just begun and I was the last to leave the vestry. As I closed the door behind me, I noticed the front row was full of visitors whom I understood to be Anglicans and Methodists – described as 'not Pentecostal orientated'!

Just as I put my foot on the steps of the platform a beautifully dressed lady and her daughter fell down on their faces. I was alarmed because I always demanded order and respect in my meetings, and still do. Performances of hysteria were never allowed in our gatherings. I rushed down to the front row to enquire what had really happened.

Those standing close exclaimed: 'Vicar, did you see him?' (In those early days I was known as 'the young vicar'; some even called me 'the young father'!)

'Who?' I asked.

'When you came into the pulpit we saw a shining figure in a long white coat with bare feet walking up the steps before you.'

And apparently as I gave out the opening hymn – He was still there!

Just as I announced the first verse, I stopped, pointed to a young mother and said: 'You tried to commit suicide today, but a voice told you to come here for you would hear words that would guide you for the rest of your life and for eternity.'

The mother cried out for mercy and was saved there and then – she was a total stranger! I looked at my watch – it was 6.35 p.m. The service was barely five minutes old, and by then the people who had fallen on the floor like cut trees had come around.

What had happened?

They said: 'We saw Him.'

'Who?'

'The Master, He's in this place and He's in you.'

I hadn't even started to preach yet. A man came up the aisle of the church. 'Vicar', he said, 'there's a power that comes on me and grips me that I can't move, help me'.

I put my hands upon him and as I touched him I

said: 'Sir, you have had a bereavement, you have buried your dear wife six months ago, but you have been so overwhelmed by grief you have gone to a spiritualist medium. She is a child of satan, and since she put her hand on you, you have been like this ever since.

'Repent of your sins, thus said the Lord, the enemy that has bound you is gone!'

The man also cried for mercy and was saved. While this was going on, I heard a scream. A woman sitting on the front row pulled back her scarf and began to point to her throat. She had had quite a sizeable goitre. During the presence of the Lord, the goitre had disappeared! Well, what can you say? There's no argument against that – the whole place was electric! The woman was healed, and no one could say anything against it, and I had nothing to do with it. I preached my message soon after that, made my appeal and many more people came to Christ. I was aware of the same power that came into Spring Street and that came upon me on the Ravenhill Road.

The Risen Christ was at work!

I returned home at Christmas were I took Gospel Meetings for the next four months. I was still only eighteen years of age.

5

Finding the centre of God's will

One January afternoon I was walking over the Albert Bridge when I saw a young mother coming toward me with her baby. Suddenly I found myself calling to her: 'Don't do it! Don't do it! Jesus loves you and will give you direction in life.' She wept, for she had been walking aimlessly from the town centre, distressed. Her husband was soon to be released from prison but she knew she had no future while he was still bound by sin. 'Lily', I said, 'I will win Sydney to Christ'. Three weeks later Sydney walked into the place where I was holding a ten day campaign – he had nothing but a pair of dungarees! When I gave the appeal, he came to Christ, and what a change! That man and his wife have been a blessing to multitudes of people and to preachers, and he has been a great soulwinner himself. His name is 'Evangelist, Sydney Murrey'.

During that ten day campaign, thirty-three people came to Christ including my only sister, Lila – which thrilled me tremendously. God was to spare her, after her terrible illness, twenty-one years; she served for many years in the Whitewell Church as a Sunday School teacher. Also at that same meeting, Robert

Gass – famed all over the United States for his television ministry – came to the Saviour.

But the time was coming when God would put me in the one place for over thirty years.

In between taking special evangelical meetings, I served as an assistant pastor to James Forsythe whose church was in the Shankill area of Belfast.

As a young man, I was having the time of my life, travelling here and there and then coming home to minister on the famous Shankill Road. Many precious souls were won to Christ at that time: it seemed God was enlarging my ministry. A long tour of Europe was arranged ending with a trip to the United States. However, little did I know that God was overruling those arrangements and planning something else. In fact it would be seventeen years before I would finally visit the United States!

Now down in the north of Belfast, there were a couple of families who wanted to start a witness in the Greencastle/Whitewell district. An approach was made to me as to whether I was interested. But I was too caught up with the idea of travelling and trying to make a name for myself. I quietly refused. Some weeks passed and I heard an approach had been made to a certain brother regarding North Belfast and he in fact was considering the matter. Now you can judge this in any way you choose, but when I heard this man was even considering going to North Belfast, I found myself being troubled.

I shrugged it off – after all I was going on tour and in my zeal and enthusiasm I was going to blaze a trail for God. Who wanted to be bothered with a few people trying to pioneer a work with very slender resources? But the Holy Spirit (speaking reverently) was concerned, and He was interested in starting something in North Belfast. I noticed my prayer times began again to lack that zip and eagerness. I knew something was wrong and put it down to my having a 'lean spell', which all Christians and ministers have. We are so good at covering up what we really feel and know when deep down in our hearts we know what we should do! And the explanations we invent to gloss over those real feelings are quite ingenious – but God is watching us all the time as we in our fickleness try to shrug off our responsibility. God has a way of dealing with every one of us. He uses His Holy Spirit to speak to us and spotlights our true sincerity or our real selfishness, and that's the way God has always dealt with me. Another showdown was coming between me and the one who had a purpose for my life.

I have always believed in the saying, 'keep short accounts with God'. In other words, don't let things or situations linger, bringing you further and further away from God. I felt there was something blocking me in my relationship with the Lord Jesus, so one afternoon I stayed indoors and refused to go out on any calls. I was down on the floor on my face, for I loved the Lord Jesus with all my heart. 'What is it Lord?' I cried. Finally the realisation came to me. My selfishness, my self-centredness and my ambition were all ruling my life so much that I had casually dismissed the very idea of going to North Belfast!

Some may interpret, and say: 'James McConnell, you really knew all the time what you should have done!' Friend, you are right! Most of us know what we should be doing but because of our plans, our ideas, our preconceived notions, we dramatise situations and blow them up out of all proportion. We really know this! But the truth is we don't want to know: it is only when we go into the inner sanctuary, into the presence of God Himself, where the Mercy Seat is covered by the precious Blood, that we understand.

I immediately knew I had to go to North Belfast, but I also knew it would not be easy, as for the next sixteen years I would be virtually buried in the

Whitewell area. The 'boy preacher' was becoming a man, and God was dealing with the man differently than He had dealt with the boy. I was going to find out the truth of Eliab's words to David when he came down to the valley of Elah with bread and cheese for his brothers and saw the Philistine giant – 'With whom hast thou left those few sheep in the wilderness?' That's where God was sending me, I thought – into the wilderness.

Like David, looking after a few sheep, following the ewes with young, listening to them, loving them, caring for them and practically carrying them! Some of them didn't know their right hand from their left. But that's where God had called me and that's where I had to be if my Master and I were to continue our relationship, because it was a love relationship: I loved the Lord Jesus with all my heart.

May I stop at this juncture and say especially to pastors and young Christian workers: instant success is rare. I hear of it, but only from time to time. If God is going to use you there must be the proving period, there must be the hard period, there must be the hidden period while others are having success and blessing. Still you are plodding on and you will wonder if it is all worth while. My word to you is: Keep praying, remain faithful, call upon God, keep your spirit sweet, don't let yourself grow sour or envious. Maybe you are right – the person near to you who is having so-called success doesn't measure up to Bible principals and standards, but that is not your concern. Your responsibility is to keep on with what God has given *you* to do. And that's the way it was with me – many times these eyes were filled with tears as year after year I laboured, with seemingly little reward.

But God knew what He was doing and where He could find me. He was chopping me and changing me bit by bit for a mighty wave of Holy Ghost conviction and soul saving in the lives of thousands of people.

The Whitewell pastorate began, and I was nineteen years and nine months old.

An unusual prophecy

As a minister of the gospel, I believe in the miraculous gifts of I Corinthians 12 and the great commission given by our Lord Jesus in Mark 16 – with signs following. But I always have had a balanced view on these gifts and tried to teach my congregation to have that same balanced attitude. I suppose many Pentecostals would class me as a critic as I am firmly convinced that most of what goes on in Pentecostal circles under the guise of spiritual gifts is imagination. The gifts exercised according to the rules laid down by the Holy Spirit in I Corinthians 14 are beautiful to behold and hear. So if I am classed as a critic I don't mind; at least I am a constructive critic, and someone has called me a Pentecostal with a small 'p'.

That first morning on 23rd February, 1957 began with a fall of snow during the night. The hall we rented was still reeking with beer smells from the night before and I remember, together with a fellow worker, brushing up the cigarette ends and opening the windows to let the smell out, and at the same time being frozen! We had ten people to start with that morning, but twelve visitors came, making the grand total of that opening service twenty-two persons.

One man, recollecting that occasion, spoke with a smile of the young skinny preacher with the Brylcream stuck on his head announcing in revolutionary language a great work that was going to start in Whitewell! We got down to business, the Scriptures were read and expounded and the Lord's Table was instituted as each of us broke bread and drank wine remembering the Lord's death. Suddenly in the midst of our worship a prophecy was given. It went something like this:

> Thus saith the Lord, you will remember this day. This day is the beginning of months, months of tears, hardship and difficulties. But if you will be faithful I will breathe upon you by my spirit and give you a people that will touch this land. This church will become a reaping church and will benefit the community so much, the people in this area will build a memorial unto you for my glory and honour. I will bring into your midst hundreds of young people and many visitors will come to you by aeroplane and ship to see what the Lord has accomplished among you . . .

I opened my eyes and looked – trying to compare what had just been said to the people that sat around the Table that morning. I tried to be honest – they were a motley bunch, and I didn't look very promising either!

Now the Scripture says: 'Prophecy is to be judged', and the only way we could judge this prophecy was to wait. If we kept the conditions – 'If you will be faithful . . . – it would come to pass.' Then, if it came to pass, it must be of the Lord!

It was of the Lord – but it took many years for it to come to fruition and it is still being fulfilled in our church today. The Holy Spirit spoke truly that morning over thirty years ago and when He speaks things come to pass in His plan and in His time. But to fulfil His plan He started slowly but surely (and if I might add painstakingly) to bring in the men and the women He would use for His purpose. When you think of it – it is incredible. When He spoke, thousands of the people to become involved weren't even born, others were far away from the Whitewell area with no notion whatsoever of ever coming near the place! But during the next thirty years, people from every walk of life – Protestant and Catholic – were being prepared, conditioned and fashioned.

Circumstances were going to be created to cause them to come into Whitewell, and in the meantime I and the little flock God had given me were to go through all sorts of phases and situations and times until the Word of the Lord would come to pass. As the prophet Habakkuk said: 'For the vision is yet for an appointed time, but at the end it shall speak, and not lie: though it tarry, wait for it; because it will surely come, it will not tarry.' (Habakkuk 2:3.)

And this is what James McConnell and the Whitewell flock had to do – to work continually with this in mind even though at times it would be very difficult indeed. To borrow Paul's words in I Timothy 1:18: 'This charge I commit unto thee, son Timothy, according to the prophecies which went before on thee, that thou by them mightest war a good warfare.'

The vision would come!

The first twelve years

Soon after this, in order to be near my flock, I moved to the Whiteabbey area where I lived on my own for about eighteen months. As one can imagine, it wasn't easy for a young man trying to take care and look after himself! The first utensil I bought was a tin opener – in fact, two, just in case I lost one!

Resources in the small church were scarce so I had to walk everywhere – but I coped! Washing and ironing proved to be quite an experience; so also was the effort to make myself look presentable. Those were days when every penny was a prisoner. I took great care over my financial affairs because I couldn't afford to make mistakes and I literally trusted God to meet my every need. That line in the Lord's Prayer held me in good stead where He taught us to pray: 'Give us this day our daily bread'.

That sort of proving and training doesn't do a minister any harm for when God prospers him, he will not easily forget the day of small things! The Holy Spirit was teaching me that if I could be faithful in the small things, one day I could be faithful in the big things! This may be your particular test: lots of men have grown weary and have disqualified themselves from that test. I say to you: Grit your teeth and get on with the job in hand.

Remember the words of Paul as found in II Corinthians 9:6: 'He that soweth sparingly shall reap sparingly, but he that soweth bountifully shall reap bountifully'. And again in Galatians 6:9: 'Let us not be weary in well doing: for in due season we shall reap, if we faint not.' I walked the roads praying, rapping doors, giving invitations, visiting hospitals; in fact, I visited anybody who was in need. But I must admit at this particular time it was hard work, it was exacting work, it was exhausting work. I was sowing, and sowing time is not always the greatest time nor the happiest time for the man of God. But I believed passionately in what I was doing. I clung to what David said speaking about the sower in Psalm 126:6: 'He that goeth forth and weepeth, bearing precious seed, shall doubtless come again with rejoicing, bringing his sheaves with him'.

During this time, I met a young lady, Margaret Foster, from one of our churches. After a short courtship, we were married in April 1959.

Through those early years Margaret proved herself a real help meet as year after year we laboured trying to make our little church strong. I appreciate Margaret for her patience and longsuffering as sometimes a dedicated man is not easy to live with – he eats, sleeps and drinks the work of God continually.

It was some thirteen years before we took our very first holiday together with our two children, Linda and Julie, and indeed it was a further year before we got our first car. I remember those times when some would say we were foolish putting the work of God and the people of God first. Maybe we were and maybe we weren't! But what we were doing was as unto the Lord. We believed He saw the motives and the intentions of our hearts. It was only after we built and opened our first Church Sanctuary in 1969 that we finally managed to get away on holiday!

So I pay tribute to my wife Margaret for her faithfulness. However, difficult as those early years were, God has made it up to her in many ways.

My two daughters Linda and Julie are adorable girls. Being 'preacher's kids' life was not easy for them, as people always expect more from them. But people forget that 'preacher's kids' are just like any other kids, they need to be loved, fed, clothed and educated. They are now grown up, and I am so proud of them in the Lord.

My oldest daughter is my private secretary: she is responsible for the administrative side of the Whitewell Church. Her husband Norman is my youth pastor and has proved himself to be a young man of tremendous ability in every aspect of God's work.

I thank God today for the family He has given me!

One incident from those early years still lives with me: my daughter Linda, then about two years old, took ill. We sent for the doctor who duly wrote a prescription to be taken to the chemist to obtain the medication she required. But there was a problem! To procure this prescription we needed two shillings and six pence, and we hadn't got the money! That's how scarce our resources were! Our first reaction was to go out and borrow the money, but I was stopped in my tracks – we were servants of God trying to do His will! I took Linda in my arms to my room, laid my hands upon her in the name of the Lord Jesus and rebuked the fever. That very same hour, she began to mend and we didn't need the medication. That prescription has lain around the house for many years. The test of scanty provisions and meagre resources that God in His wisdom allowed us to go through equipped us for the days that would lie ahead.

We had nothing. In fact we were nothing. But God's hand was upon us, for little did I know He would put into my hand, during the next twenty years, literally hundreds of thousands of pounds! Even to this day, we are still careful with every penny God gives us and brings us.

Maybe there is a servant of God reading this, and at this moment you feel a failure and insignificant. In fact, there have been occasions when you feel you are wasting your time, your flock's time and the Lord's time! Don't give up! Tell your Master about it; remember the words of Paul regarding servants of God in Romans 14:4: 'To his own Master he standeth or falleth'. Go out for a walk somewhere, talk out loud, tell your Master how you feel, ask Him to give you the grace you need until your particular harvest comes in.

As I write this, I feel I know what you are going through. One notable day, whilst walking home from the centre of the city in the snow (I couldn't afford the bus fare), I was feeling wretched, my faith was down. I recall blurting out loudly to the Lord: 'Father, if you just want me to look after these seventy people you have given me for the rest of my life, then I bow to your will, I will love and spoil them!'

I believe God in His grace and mercy heard that pitiable outburst and tenderly smiled at me. He knew He was going to multiply those seventy exceedingly!

8

A house for the Lord

As time passed by it became evident that we as a Church would not get anywhere until we had a spiritual home of our own where we could have extra meetings, where we could train young people and establish facilities suitable for young children.

The place we rented was not suitable, if we were ever to get Roman Catholics in under the sound of the gospel. The by-laws of the hall stated that Roman Catholics were not allowed into these particular premises, although at times, we are delighted to say, Catholics unaware of this came in and were saved. But we needed a place of our own, although we were grateful for the twelve years we were in that hall.

Soon ground was purchased and plans were passed and under way. All the brethren of the church, young and old, started to work on the foundations of the site, but problems began to raise their heads! As our building site was literally a hill, it had to be excavated; the excavators went so close to the adjoining property that the owners panicked, threatening a court order because their property was in danger of collapsing.

Our architect had immediately to design a large retaining wall to go right around the site in order to protect the property. This was in late 1966, and the cost of this retaining wall was over twenty-five hundred pounds – a small fortune in those days, and quite a sizeable sum for seventy people to raise who were trying to build a church.

We had to hire contractors to build this solid wall of concrete, going down over twelve feet to the foundations. The only way now to move that wall is to use explosives! But alas! When the account came in, some of my members became alarmed and made all sorts of excuses and left.

I was left with forty adults and ten children. How now could this building be raised?

For a few months we were devastated and saw only this large retaining wall with the foundations partly dug. But in six months we gathered ourselves together, and those forty people during the next two years raised, above our church expenses, thirty thousand pounds!

Every day our brethren were there from early morning to late at night with a brother John McAllister supervising the work. The giving and sacrifice of those forty people, and their labours, were outstanding! We were determined by the grace of God to build a house totally sanctified to His service.

It would take a large book to record the fantastic ways God met our needs and encouraged us. As for myself, I literally dug in that building site for two years, digging, mixing cement, carrying bricks and doing deals with sub-contractors to get the best price. This was all new to me but it was another phase God was leading me into – teaching me many things. Some nights I would literally drop into bed and when it was time to get up the next morning I could only open my eyes but couldn't move my body. God was teaching me what Christ said to the Ephesian Church in Revelation 2:2: 'I know thy labour'. The Greek word used here for labour is *kopos*, which means 'toil that exhausts'. Over the next few years I was to experience that time and time again!

Once again I say: If you want to be a success for

God, you have got to learn to work with everything you've got.

If you are not prepared to work hard, forget about the ministry – you'll never achieve anything! Is it not significant that the Lord Jesus declared in John 5:17: 'My Father worketh hitherto and I work'? And if Christ and His Father worked together how much more should we!

Finally on 5th April 1969 with great rejoicing we entered our new building. It had a small balcony, and could seat 450 people.

When you think of the twelve years we were in that rented hall, this building was like a cathedral to us. We were delighted with our new spiritual home and God brought more new people in with souls being saved nearly every month.

Then the 'troubles' really broke out in Ulster. The scene for the next eighteen years was one of violence, assassination, and bombing. On two occasions there were gun battles outside the church between terrorists and the army, and imbedded in the ceiling of the church are bullets which are still there after all these years.

One August day when we were going away with the children on a Sunday School outing, we were told by the police to be sure and come home early as they had heard our church might be blown up by terrorists. You can imagine how we felt, after all these years of labour, to be told that after only four months in our new home it might be razed to the ground. We asked what protection could be given, and the reply was 'Very little', as the security forces were under severe pressure, being stretched. Anger came over us. We simply would not allow this to happen, and that night our brethren slept in the church watching and getting prepared for an attack. We had sand, hoses and water all at the ready, but the night passed peacefully.

Another incident remains in my memory. It was a

Friday night and my youth leader, Leslie Lyons (now a successful missionary in Spain, pastoring four churches, having started in Benidorm with three people in 1975) was holding a prayer meeting in one of the rooms of the church. During the prayer meeting a gun battle commenced outside the church. I was alarmed and ran all the way down the Whitewell Road. A nervous young soldier shouted at me, his gun raised to my head: 'Stop where you are!' I explained to him that a number of young people were in the church and I was the pastor. Would he let me pass to find out if they were all right? He graciously did!

When I entered the church, much to my surprise there were about fifteen young people praying. Twelve of them had been baptised in the Holy Spirit during the gun battle and one of them was my daughter Linda. Leslie Lyons said they never heard what was going on outside! Which shows that when a person is in the Spirit, the peace of God can garrison his heart at all times. It reminded me of what David said in Psalm 27:5: 'For in the time of trouble He shall hide me in his pavilion: in the secret of His tabernacle shall He hide me; He shall set me up upon a rock.'

There have been events in these Troubles that never have been published or recorded – would to God they were! Christ would be glorified. All the Press want to glorify is hypocrisy and violence and that is what makes the news.

Those early days of the Troubles were fraught with danger as we lived in a mixed community and our church was right in the centre. Today the area where our church is situated is 75% Roman Catholic and we get on very well with our neighbours.

But in those days, as occasionally now, there were times when you could cut the atmosphere with a knife. As the years passed it was my sad task to officiate at the funerals of many of those who had suffered during the violence – some assassinated by their own men.

At times – and this still happens now – my telephone would ring during the night, and voices – male and female – would threaten me, telling me what they would do to me if I didn't stop preaching. But I saw the hypocrisy of politicians, even ministers of religion and the Catholic hierarchy, and I spoke against all the establishment.

The Church of Jesus Christ should be giving a clear cut direction to the people of God and eventually to their nation. But the Church was strangely silent! Yes – the Church condemned the murder and the brutality. It was like a record or listening to a tape recording! 'We abhor this dastardly deed.' Surely, I thought, if God's people were blood-washed and spirit-filled, we could do something for our land!

But James McConnell – what was he doing? He was just as bad! An armchair politician! A minister saying all the right things and occasionally being in danger, but totally ineffective!

A wave of discontent and restlessness came over me. I found myself going out for long walks, walking for miles, calling upon God, asking Him, in His grace, to anoint me by His Spirit. I went out walking even in the rain, many a time stopped at two or three in the morning by the police or army asking what I was up to!

They got to know me and sometimes even to this day if I am out late and there's tension, a police Land-Rover will pick me up and bring me home much to my frustration!

Every child of God has a way and a method to pray and from a boy I used to walk and pray and feel that I had touched God and God touched me. I still do this even now at fifty years of age.

I see now some of my young men in Whitewell who are entering the ministry doing the same thing on many occasions. Many a time I have passed by, unknown to them, seeing the earnestness and determination on their faces. While Ulster has young men of this calibre there's a glorious future for our country – not as the religious and political backwater that crystal ball politicians in Westminster are predicting!

As I said, I pounded the beat, praying and crying unto God. Then I became restless with Whitewell. The meetings were good, solid and sound – how these expressions cover up our failure. The people were loyal enough but content just to attend on Sundays and to go home. They enjoyed my visits, looked forward to me coming and were kind to me. But we were getting nowhere, we were on the 'Magic Roundabout'!

After days of prayer, I got up one Sunday morning and made this announcement: 'Brothers and sisters, I love you, but you are settled, contented and happy. Surely that's all a minister would want in his church. But you don't want to be bothered to reach out.'

Whitewell at that time could have been classed as an average Pentecostal Church. For instance, at the morning service we broke bread and remembered the Lord's death. The usual three people spoke with tongues having three interpretations and an odd prophecy thrown in! How dreadful – it was all so boring!

I hope this statement doesn't offend any Pentecostal pastor reading this; but if such a pastor honestly sits down and analyses the whole situation he will see that I was right!

The Monday night prayer meeting, with its forty people attending, with six persons monopolising the prayer time by praying nearly ten minutes each, with a talk in tongues now and again. I cried: 'Is this God? Is this the Holy Ghost? Is this first century Christianity? If it is, then there's something seriously wrong with me!'

So that morning I said: 'Once again, brothers and sisters, I love you. However, God has not called me to be a keeper of an aquarium, but a fisher of men.'

I saw them look at each other but I continued.

'I will visit you when you are sick and in real need and when you are in hospital. But since you are content and not willing to bring people in, I will endeavour to do so myself, by God's help. You will find me rapping the doors of all kinds of political and religious persons.'

One man came to me afterwards and said: 'James, we love your ministry, don't get yourself heated up, things will work themselves out, you don't need to rap doors!'

That statement from him revealed how totally complacent he really was! But I was determined!

Week after week saw me, much to the annoyance of some of my members, walking the streets – knocking doors, introducing myself to all sort and types of people. I must admit I was enjoying every moment of it! The varied experiences I had were extremely interesting. Sometimes I would be in the home of a person who was dying, offering comfort and leading that person to Christ. Eventually some member of that family would start coming to Whitewell, hearing the word and getting saved. This is what it was all about!

Once I remember calling at a home where a lady was having a baby – all on her own! I made her a cup of tea, filled a water bottle to keep her warm – then panicked and quickly telephoned the doctor! Again, members of her family started to come to Whitwell.

I recall another time when I called at a house where a group of men were sitting over a drink discussing religion and politics (a usual topic in Ulster). I was brought in and allowed to engage in the discussion – throwing in my 'ten cents' about what the Lord Jesus could do for every one of them. The remarkable thing was their children started to come to the church.

Another incident that stands out in my mind was a bereavement in a home where I had been visiting and witnessing. I went to the funeral to offer my condol-

ences, only to find that the minister had forgotten to
come – much to the consternation of the family. I was
asked there and then to take the funeral service both
in the home and at the cemetery. My presence there
was appreciated, and loved ones of that family came
to Whitewell. By God's grace I seemed to pop up everywhere where I would be needed!

At other times doors were closed in my face and I
was curtly told: 'We are not interested'. But it was
worth it all. People were slowly coming in from every
walk of life – Catholic and Protestant alike. But I
knew this was only a trickle – God was wanting to do
more!

I was still tramping the roads seeking the Lord's
face. Then, I thought, God must move through the
Whitewell Church. I must motivate them to seek the
Lord.

So once again I got up on another Lord's Day
morning and announced: 'There will be prayer meetings indefinitely – in fact until God moves. Starting
Monday to Thursday each evening at 8 p.m., with
another prayer meeting on Tuesday morning at 10
a.m.' Sometimes on a late Friday afternoon or night
the church deacons would meet together with me for
prayer. Prayer meetings are better than board/busi-
ness meetings. Board/business meetings usually
become 'bored meetings'.

That meant there were six prayer meetings each
week at Whitewell. I preached on Sunday mornings
and evenings and one could even feel the spiritual
temperature rising in the Whitewell Church as
brothers and sisters were getting gripped by the Holy
Ghost.

These prayer meetings went on for two and a half
years, non-stop!

My theme midweek was: 'We are closed for repairs'
– until God in His grace could finally deal with our

hearts. And He did! He was dealing with mine and intensifying my hunger for Him.

Sometimes I honestly think that some churches should 'close for repairs' until God visits them. But how vague and naive some pastors are. They think: Call a top evangelist from somewhere, book him for a two-week revival. But revival doesn't come through top evangelists – nor what they have in their brief-cases. Revival comes from the presence of God!

'Pastor McConnell, does prayer bring revival?' My reply: 'It helps!' But it doesn't bring revival; revival is a sovereign work of the Holy Spirit. But what constant prayer does is this: it puts a man, it puts a woman, it puts a church into a real spiritual relationship with God. It puts one on speaking terms with God – for many professing Christians these days are not!

But the principal thing that prayer does is this: it causes a man, woman or a church to become available in the sight of God. If he wants a job done or a situation attended to – He has the necessary vessels or instruments to perform the task.

By this time the Troubles had reached their peak. Violence, bloodshed and bombing were the order of the day.

In fact, some of our members couldn't get to church because buses were being hi-jacked and burned. Those of our members who were living in 'flashpoint' areas were frightened to come out. This was how and why our Bus Ministry began. We bought our first bus to call for people who normally came to church, but extra people came and the bus was packed. Then we received a gift of £1,600 to purchase another bus. Soon it, too, was full; and today we have thirty-five large buses on the road with a full time garage manager and five faithful, fantastic workers to keep the wheels running.

During this particular time, in one of our prayer meetings, the Holy Spirit spoke through prophecy in a special way. He said two things were required of us as a people, and if we were obedient He would make the house we were now in totally inadequate for the people who would come! Those two things were faithfulness and courage; and at all times the 'doors of this house' must be kept open at all costs, no matter what happened. And if we were faithful God would be faithful. That word was written on our hearts.

But what was happening to me? I was still hungry for God; some days I parked my car a couple of streets away and locked myself in the church, crying unto the Lord.

Then during the month of September 1973, something took place which turned my life upside down.

One afternoon while in prayer, I was strangely aware of a mighty presence. I was afraid, but my fear disappeared as I recognised the same light that visited me in 14 Spring Street and on the Ravenhill Road. Out of that mighty presence I was given the knowledge that souls were to be saved every week, and that each time we would endeavour to do something for the gospel and with the gospel, God would in His grace confirm His word.

Over the next few weeks I felt as if my heart was breaking. An overwhelming sense of God's presence dissolved me in tears time and time again. Looking back at it all – God by the power of the Holy Spirit was breaking up the fallow ground in my life. I didn't share this with my people until six months later. I believed if God had visited me and done a great work of grace in my life, others would see it. My older members can tell you that during those early days I was inclined to be hard in my dealings with others and unadaptable. But with that visit I was given love that I never had before.

Many times my brethren and friends would wait on the inevitable out-burst – but it never came! In those days, the Holy Spirit had turned me inside out. But

from that September afternoon, every week without
fail, men and women were coming to Jesus Christ.

On many occasions while in prayer, the Holy Spirit
would whisper in my ear the name and address of
some man or woman whom I had never seen before in
my life. I would go and visit them, telling them to
their amazement and to my own that God had sent
me!

I was staggered to realise how many unsaved people
and Christian people were in great need, seeking God,
seeking assurance and looking for a word from God –
and here I was giving them that word. It also began
to happen in the service – strangers came in, were
spoken to and given direction. Some were healed and
many were saved. One lady who had been told that
eventually she would be in a wheelchair came in and
got saved, and a 'Thus saith the Lord' was pronounced
– she never was to use that wheelchair. That was eight
years ago!

Then one Sunday morning a prophecy was given.
Prophecies in Whitewell were few and far between,
but when they were given, people listened, for they
knew the Holy Spirit was present.

The spoken word went like this: 'Have you love?
Prepare yourselves for I am going to bring to you those
that live in the dunghill, those that are the offscouring
of society. Receive them, love them as I have received
and loved you.'

Almost immediately that word took place – what
a host assembled! Terrorists, alcoholics, prostitutes,
divorcees, drug addicts, homosexuals – both Catholic
and Protestant.

It became like the Cave of Adullam – everyone that
was in distress, everyone that was in debt, everyone
that was discontented came and the Lord Jesus
became a Captain over them. The place was packed.
First we pulled out the balcony and extended it to a
hundred seats. That was filled in two weeks. Then we

knocked down one wall and made room for a further one hundred and ten persons. Again in two weeks that was filled! We knocked down the other wall and got another one hundred people in. We could do no more. Seven hundred people were literally crammed in to that house – almost to suffocation.

The foyer, the very toilets were full of people. God was moving by His spirit.

9

The critics

Of course a move of God is not without criticism and slander. Many taunts were levelled against us as to the type of people we were allowing into our church. But what our critics didn't realise was that what was happening was also new to us. We were a conventional little Pentecostal church and we hadn't the machinery or the facilities to cope with the fish that were caught in our net. We were to learn by trial and error. The church became full of problems, but they were 'not problems of death', but rather 'problems of life'. We learned you don't clean fish before you catch them – you catch them first, then clean them!

Under this lovely wave of the Holy Spirit, catching was somewhat easy, but cleaning was another matter and we needed all the patience and understanding we had.

It reminded me of what Alan Redpath said in his book on the making of a man of God: 'The conversion of a soul is the miracle of a moment. The manufacturing of a saint is the task of a life time.'

There is no doubt many of these people were soundly saved. But it took a number of years for some of them to be rehabilitated and to become members of the church and today they are the finest Christians you could meet.

What was it our Lord said to Simon the Pharisee in

Luke 7:47 when the woman who was a sinner washed His holy feet with her tears and wiped them with the hairs of her head? He said: 'Wherefore I say unto thee, her sins, which are many, are forgiven; for she loved much; but to whom little is forgiven, the same loveth little.'

That's what was happening all around us. But were the conversions genuine? Time would tell!

We reminded ourselves that the precious seed fell on four kinds of ground: the wayside, the stony, the thorny and the good. It seemed one in every four grew to maturity (Mark 4:14–20).

Also we remembered the words of our Lord in Matthew 13:47–48: 'The Kingdom of Heaven is like unto a net, that was cast into the sea, and gathered of every kind: which, when it was full, they drew to shore, and sat down, and gathered the good into vessels, but cast the bad away.'

The apostle Paul in 1 Corinthians 12 and in Ephesians 1 describes Christ's blood-washed people as the Church which is His Body. Christ is the Head, we are the Body. Speaking with all reverence, we can say that we are His arms, His legs, His feet, His hands. What would Christ have done to the poor souls who came in through our doors – but receive them!

The church should also be a hospital; in fact our members smilingly call our buses 'the Whitewell ambulances' – bringing sin-sick souls to God's house!

Christ didn't form a glorified social club, nor a fur coat brigade nor a *Who's Who* centre. He said in Matthew 28:19: 'Go ye therefore, and make disciples of all nations, baptising them in the Name of the Father and the Son and the Holy Ghost, teaching them to observe all things which I have commanded you.'

This is the Church's job, and if we are not doing it then we are only playing!

10

Another new house

Whitewell was growing, and growing strong. We sent out Leslie and Brenda Lyons to Spain in 1975, where they ministered for a year to three people in Benidorm. Today they have four good churches in Spain reaching precious souls for Christ. Also Whitewell was involved behind the Iron Curtain sending finances and material needs to evangelical believers who were suffering there. In fact, it was my privilege to make a trip there, smuggling Bibles, food, clothes and money.

No matter what man of God came to the church, he was helped and encouraged. But it soon became apparent we were going to lose our growth if we didn't increase our physical capacity to cope with new people.

So we began to pray for a new Sanctuary, and the next few years from October 1978 to October 1981 were a mixture of blessings and wonders, with hundreds of souls being saved, and great hardship and trial.

God always tries or tests His people, and He will continue to do so.

The church gave me leave to negotiate for a piece of land. What do I mean by saying the church gave me 'leave'? Simply this: Whitewell has always been the people's church. The church naturally has a Board of Trustees and Deacons – but only in the name of the people. I personally was in an unique position, being

the local founder of the local church and beginning as
the pastor of the church on the same day the church
began. So I always went to the people!

I believe in God's plan that there should be elders
in the church. But these elders are not ornaments, nor
are they little tin gods – they should be men of love
and inspiration who lead by example. But men like
that are as scarce as hen's teeth these days!

The purchasing of the ground is a story in itself.
But we got ground and told the planning authorities
that we wanted to build a Sanctuary seating 1,500
persons.

After much debate the authorities said that in prin-
ciple they had no objections to our plan, but that we
would need a car park. There was a piece of land
adjoining ours on which there was a large old house
with a driveway. I approached the (then) owner of the
land: the sum he asked for was a colossal amount,
and I was happy there was a delay in the planning
department in order to give us a respite to gather the
money. (That is the only time I was ever happy that
the planning department was slow! They reminded me
of that verse in Genesis, when the Lord made 'all
creeping things'.)

Meanwhile the owner of the ground sold out. One
morning, after prayer, I was putting on my tie when
suddenly the Presence of the Lord came into my
bedroom and said: 'Prepare yourself today. A man is
coming to meet you concerning the ground – offer him
£15,000.' I was staggered! I couldn't concentrate on my
work all day. I finally came home well before lunch
time and stayed in the entire afternoon.

Time went by. Was I imagining what I heard that
morning?

I was watching the six o'clock news when the door
bell rang. It was the owner of the ground. He asked if
I was interested. My reply: 'Most certainly!'

He said he was willing to sell to me for £18,000. I

replied, 'I have been told to give you £15,000.' He said: 'Who told you?' I just answered: 'Headquarters'!

We discussed some practical problems, and finally we shook hands. I had agreed that inside one month I would give him £15,000 – and we hadn't one penny!

The next night I told the people – they were thrilled! We set two weeks aside for the Lord to meet this financial need.

On the given Sunday, the Whitewell people gave £18,000, three thousand above what was needed!

I ran into the planning department's offices, told them I had purchased land for a car park – and the plans were duly passed!

So far, so good.

11

Miscellaneous events

I remember vividly when we were preparing the site for the digger to come and scoop out our basement. A large towering tree stood in the middle of the property. I felt sad because the tree would have to be cut down! It looked so majestic, so lovely – yet when we felled it, upon examination, we discovered it was rotten inside! What a lesson that tree was to teach me during the next eight years to follow – about myself and about people. It looked good, it looked lovely, it looked the part. But inside there was decay, there was rottenness and there was defect. I said to the young men who helped me fell that particular tree: 'Brethren, may we never be like this piece of wood – outwardly beautiful but corrupt inside!'

That should be the story of our lives before God – we should from time to time examine ourselves; or, better still, let Him examine us. As David cried in Psalm 139:23–24: 'Search me, O God, and know my heart; try me, and know my thoughts: and see if there be any wicked way in me, and lead me in the way everlasting.'

It is strange how things are written on your mind and how they never leave it!

That particular day, my daughter Julie's cat, Darkie, presented us with four kittens! We had called the cat Darkie because we thought she was a he!

Everything about that day combined to teach me that appearances can prove false!

Soon, once again, together with my colleagues and my congregation, I was digging foundations and mixing cement – back to my old job! My close friend Bertie Blake and I remember how at times we were so stuck in the mud and rain that each time we lifted our feet, we left our boots in the mud, and were left standing in our stocking soles! The fellowship was good, the comradeship of those brethren was fantastic as we laboured day after day. Indeed that time of building cemented friendships for ever and brought the church closer together.

We erected that great house in three years. As we look back how we managed to do this was only a miracle from God. He was in His work: Whitewell was in His plan no matter what obstacle or criticism was placed before us.

As before, John McAllister supervised the work. What a splendid man he is! He will always be appreciated in Whitewell.

The forming and building of the basement actually took us longer than the erecting of the Sanctuary. Regulations demanded that every rule was to be obeyed, and we did just that.

We were out to build a house that would seat one thousand five hundred people, and believed that God would give us the one thousand five hundred people!

Critics said: 'The days of big churches are over – small churches are better, people can get closer in smaller churches and there's more warmth and closeness in a small church.' Well, that may be true in many respects, but I refused to believe that in smaller churches people got close in any helpful way. I remember my days in smaller churches: when people got close, they knew everyone's business and private lives. To me that was obnoxious!

Also I remember the cliques in smaller churches,

and the usual two or three dominating families who controlled the place and the pastor for years; and the next pastor, and the next and the next! Having said that, I always bear in mind that Whitewell for many years was a small church!

The tag of 'the big church' troubled me. I constantly asked God to make Whitewell a big family, a loving family and a caring family. Surely my task as a leader is not only to motivate and inspire people, but to keep people together and to keep the unity of the church. There have been times in the Whitewell Church when two feuding families have lifted up their heads to push forward their opposing ideas and ideologies. But as a leader I have to consider *all* the people who come to listen to my ministry. I keep reminding myself that Whitewell is Christ's work, that it has been built with sweat, tears and sacrifice and that I am God's instrument to keep that work unified and to keep it growing. So I ask the feuding families either to settle down or to find themselves another church!

That may sound harsh. But as I look on it I'm in God's business of 'catching men' and preparing men for the greatest event in history: namely, the Second Coming of the Lord Jesus Christ.

Why allow some selfish, self-centred, feuding individuals to divert you from your mission? Deal with them accordingly – in love, of course. That's one of the tasks of the Christian leader.

Week by week, month by month, the house began to rise and the bills kept coming in. But God was beautifully gracious and met every need. I couldn't understand the attitude of my critics: 'They will never do it, it's too big – it costs too much money. This man and his cronies are too big for their boots!'

I have discovered that if a project, if a mission, is of God, whether it costs one pound or one million pounds – God will meet it.

One cold winter morning after the foundations and

basement had been built (and were incidentally covered in snow) one man patronisingly stated: 'Well brother, that's quite an achievement. If God stopped blessing you here and now you couldn't complain!' I looked at him in surprise and replied: 'God doesn't work like that – He's the Alpha and Omega, the Beginning and the End. What He begins, He finishes.' And God would finish this Whitewell House for His glory!

To make an incredibly long story short – the giving of the Whitewell people was magnificent. They gave their money, they gave of themselves – never has there been a people like them! Their love, their loyalty and their faithfulness, in spite of criticism, rumour, slander and hurt were unbelievable! I love them for how they stood with me and by me and as long as I live (be it long or short) I would like to stand by them, as long as God in His grace keeps annointing me and using me for His glory and kingdom.

There came a time during the building programme when we had no money left. Some of us thought it prudent to give ourselves respite for one year and then start again.

But 75% of my brethren were unemployed – that's why we had such a response every day at the building site. Their wives were glad to get them out of the house! They were there from 9.30 a.m. until 9.30 p.m. and indeed at times until midnight. In fact, some of the men on shift work began their voluntary stint at the building site at midnight!

We tried to think things out seriously. If we waited a year, a further £80,000 would be added to the cost of the building through inflation. Our decision was, therefore, to continue.

I worked it out. We needed at least £250,000 to finish the job in hand – that is, carpeting and painting the place from top to bottom (the pulpit area, offices, ante-rooms, basement, etc.); and woodwork, kitchen, lighting and seating (theatre seats), together with a new organ and piano.

The bank was willing to grant us the loan – noting our track record over the past five years. Our offerings had increased out of all proportion year by year. 'No problem,' said the bank manager; but the group to which we were affiliated refused to give their consent. They said we could only have £100,000. However, we took it because we were entitled to it, as for eleven years Whitewell had been in the black and all the interest of the Whitewell monies had gone to the Extension Fund of those who were building churches.

I then went with my colleague, Pastor Blake, to a loan company and borrowed another £100,000, placed it for a few weeks in a special account, and made enough interest on it to pay a few big bills.

If you remember, our Lord rebuked the man with the one talent not only for laziness but because he didn't get interest on it! And when the time came I drew out the money to pay for theatre seats and furnishings. We still owed about £50,000 on the beautiful stained glass windows.

But try to imagine our hearts then! We wanted this Sanctuary beautiful and comfortable for all time, for us, our children and our grandchildren, if Jesus tarried.

We wanted our children to say: 'At least our mothers and fathers had vision and loved the Lord Jesus with all their hearts; enough to try and build Him a house where His gospel would be preached.'

I made a deal with all the building firms concerning materials, asking them for special terms and promising them at certain times and certain months, I would pay them.

Counting up on the day of opening, we owed the staggering sum of well over £300,000. I tried not to think about it, but literally trusted God for each day. One particular critic said about me that either I was a complete fool or a man of faith – for I didn't know when I was beaten. Also I had been kicked so hard and so often I wouldn't know any more when I was being kicked!

To the glory of Our Lord Jesus Christ, in less than three years we had every bill paid, the finance company paid and the bank paid! Every one of those we kept waiting we paid interest, or made it up to them, to show our genuine regard and sincerity.

During those three years we brought two more men into full-time service, and increased our bus fleet, thus employing another two mechanics for the garage we had obtained. We stepped up our missionary endeavours. Indeed, Whitewell was now in a new phase, a phase that would astound us as well as other people, because the Holy Spirit had a mind to work and a mind to bless.

Once again I began to use the old methods that had served me well in the earlier days.

We were now in our new sanctuary.

After the opening services, having various guests and visitors, the church was packed. But the novelty of the new building began to wear off. I and my seven hundred and fifty faithful Whitewellers began to build the *spiritual* house. The ground floor of the building was regularly filled, but the gallery was empty. The house had to be filled; so midweek we closed again for 'repairs'! We began to seek the Lord – Tuesdays, Wednesdays, Thursdays and also Fridays when we could get together. You see, there is something on every night and every day at Whitewell! How could we get people in?

Pray them in! Invite them in! Will them in! Compel them to come in!

On Lord's Day both morning and evening, we had two great preaching services and souls were continually saved. Let me tell you, from September 1973 until this present day, we have never had *one* unfruitful

week! For over fourteen years, without fail, souls have
been saved in Whitewell. In fact, we did a survey and
discovered that over 90% of the Whitewell membership were actually saved in Whitewell.

The prophet Jeremiah said: 'Stand ye in the way
and see and ask for the old paths.' The old paths are
the best! The old paths are the truest! The old paths
are the safest if you want to be sure!

Whitewell has always been like David when he was
brought into Saul's tent to try on Saul's armour, thus
to face Goliath.

David had difficulty in moving, for we are told: 'He
assayed to go'. He turned to Saul and said: 'I cannot
go with these for I have not proved them.' But what
had he proved? He had proved the anointing of God
in his life, the communion with God in the Bethlehem
hills as he tended his father's sheep with his staff and
slingshot.

And so it was with myself and the Whitewell people.
We had proved the power of prayer and the faithfulness of prayer and the necessity of prayer.

I constantly teach the Whitewell people, 'Praying
time is never wasted time!'

> No prayer – no power.
> Less prayer – less power.
> More prayer – more power.

It took us at least six months to settle in the big
house with all its facilities. But little did we realise
that soon this big house would become alarmingly
inadequate for us as God again began to move by the
power of His Spirit.

I want at this point to tell of one incident which
happened one year before we opened the great Sanctuary. My reason for highlighting this incident is that
out of sorrow and tragedy, Christ was glorified.

David Purse (senior), one of the original ten people
who started with me in February 1957, was an Elder

and my Sunday School Superintendent for twenty-two
years. He, along with his wife and family, were
faithful members and workers of the church. David
was also in the reserve police, and one fatal Saturday
afternoon whilst on duty outside Crusaders Football
Stadium, he was cowardly and brutally shot by IRA
gunmen.

The news of the tragedy stunned the entire church.
His wife, Ann, and his three boys were wonderful!

The day of the funeral saw thousands attending.
There were more outside the church than those who
could get in. They came in their hundreds even to the
graveside where they heard the gospel. David's oldest
son (called after him) was then only fifteen years old.

But in the month of July, during a prayer meeting,
the Spirit of God moved mightily and singled out
young David Purse publicly. He was called by
prophecy to prepare himself for a work God would call
him to. At that time, David was just a young boy who
came to the Whitewell church.

That night, David went home, and (in his own
words) when he walked out of his room the next
morning, he had become a man! He said: 'It was like
young Samuel's experience at Shiloh when he heard
the voice of God.' (Samuel was but twelve years of age
at that time). David Purse is now one of the most up-
and-coming preachers in the United Kingdom and is
now pastoring our Newry church.

Out of chaos and confusion, sorrow and death, God
brought order and glorified His name. Ann and her
three boys are still with us and we are proud of them.
Their story, during that time, is only one of many of
the families at Whitewell – it seemed God was giving
us a unique church with members who had constitutions as strong as oxen.

There was also the Walker family. They had been
with me many years. The husband, Ivan, was not
saved but was a good man. One day while working on

a roof-top (he was a roofer by trade) he was shot nine times by the IRA.

Miraculously, he was still breathing. He lay unconscious in hospital for nine weeks, firstly on a life support machine, then in the intensive care unit. Many a night, late, even at two o'clock in the morning, I would drive to the Royal Victoria Hospital just to be near him and talk with him, in a vain hope that he might hear me in his unconscious state! But Christ met Ivan when he was in the coma for, as his story goes, he found himself taken by the hand into the presence of God, and a voice said: 'Father, I present Ivan Walker to you, will you receive him?' Immediately, Ivan felt the cleansing Blood of Jesus and was forgiven of his sins. Almost immediately, after that, Ivan recovered consciousness and came back into the land of the living.

The terrorists had tried to destroy him, and whilst Ivan can't continue in his business and do many things he would like to do, he still drives a car, and witnesses to Roman Catholics on the Falls Road and Springfield Road, telling them that Christ loves them and that he loves them.

These are examples of the kind of people it is my privilege to work amongst in Whitewell!

Meanwhile in Whitewell, after that season of protracted prayer, the great house began to be filled! Row after row of the gallery slowly but surely was occupied until we were frightened that there were so many people in the gallery it would surely collapse!

One week stands out in my memory: I asked all our people, starting from myself, to bring one person with them to church. They did! The church couldn't hold them; people were everywhere that night. Eighty adults came to Christ; the following week another forty and the next week twenty-five. Souls were being saved every week, but not in those numbers. It was

becoming slowly evident to me that this house was
going to be too small!

We did a small extension job by lowering the gallery
a few feet to house yet another one hundred people.
Inside two weeks, it was packed. It was the same story
all over again. So where would we go from here?
Where?

God would take us to the land's largest auditorium
and football stadium!

12

The media – television, radio and press!

We reached Christmas 1983 and found the BBC wanted to do an interview. They wanted to know why so many people were coming to the church and why so many Roman Catholics and terrorists were coming in and getting saved, and then joining the church. We didn't realise that during the next year we would again be on national television four times, and that various newspapers and periodicals would be featuring articles about what God was doing.

The Whitewell people found it difficult to take all this in, as we were so used to being criticised and ridiculed. It was quite strange to us all.

As I write this chapter, the BBC are again doing a documentary on my ministry and the effect the Whitewell Church is having on the community.

The only possible explanation for all of this is that God, by His grace and wisdom, is allowing the Whitewell Church this publicity so that others might hear the gospel, as the inhabitants of the city of Capernaum did in Mark 2. It is recorded of our Lord Jesus that He entered a house. Mark goes on to say: 'And it was noised that He was in the house. And straightway many were gathered together, insomuch that there was no room to receive them, no, not so much as about the door: and he preached the word unto them.'

We have been told that as far afield as Australia, Canada and the USA television pictures have been shown of the Whitewell witness. Truly this is the Lord's doing and it is marvellous in our eyes. But let me say this so-called publicity has had no adverse effect on the Whitewell congregation. They are still the faithful, humble people they have always been, and we are still a family church – only the family is getting bigger!

As the days passed, many changes for the good took place in the church. Growth and blessing was on every hand! God by His grace was saving 'key people' (if I might use the term) and bringing more people in to help us make His work better and to strengthen the witness.

As I have already said, we were affiliated to a certain group for a number of years. But we found it more and more difficult to stay among them as we differed doctrinally and in our outreach – evangelically and missionary-wise.

We stayed because of human relationships and sentiments, because I had grown up with these men and loved them. But eventually, I had to withdraw.

Whitewell, because of its vision and its faith and its strong emphasis on the gospel, had always been on its own.

But now Whitewell was on its own *officially*! The only difference was that we had now acknowledged what unofficially we had been for years: different in doctrine and practice from those we had tried to work with. God again by His wisdom was preparing us for greater things. But we didn't know it yet.

In the autumn of 1984, one Lord's Day morning, during the singing, I was standing with my pastors on the front row worshipping God, when a powerful desire came upon me to seek the face of the Lord.

Once again, I began to tramp the roads, calling upon the Lord, asking Him to anoint me, to cleanse me and to sanctify me, so that if He should need me, I would be available. I brought to my remembrance instances in Scripture like that in Genesis 22:1, when God called Abraham, and he replied: 'Behold, here I am'. And of Ananias the disciple in the city of Damascus we are told in Acts 9:10 that the Lord spoke to him in a vision, calling his name – Ananias – and he said: 'Behold, I am here Lord'. Again, in I Samuel 3:10, when God revealed Himself to the boy Samuel we are told: 'And the Lord came, and stood, and called as at other times, Samuel, Samuel. Then Samuel answered, Speak; for thy servant heareth.'

Each one of those men were available. I wanted to show the Lord I was available to do anything He wanted me to do. These men were in the right place at the right time and where God could find them. I too wanted to be in the right place at the right time and where God could find me.

The desire to seek Him was even stronger than in my earlier days, and I realised God was dealing with me in a new way.

I was now a man. A man nearing his fifties. A mature man, I hoped; a seasoned man. I was conscious that 'to whom much is given, of the same shall much be required'. I walked for miles and found myself meeting my church members on various roads. They stopped me, hooted their horns, waved at me as they passed by in the car. They knew I was seeking God and they were pleased. But I tried to find new 'trysting places' where I could call upon the Lord without the telephone buzzing or the doorbell ringing and where they didn't see me!

I remember this incident well. We held a Sunday night Healing Service. Our church does not give prominence to healing, but as God leads we have from time to time a Healing Service and prepare ourselves

carefully for such a ministry. The service was to start
at seven o'clock. But at six o'clock, one hour before the
commencement, the church was packed.

That night sixty persons came to Christ and many
men and women testified to the touch of God in their
bodies. The benediction was pronounced that night at
11.45 p.m. What God did that night encouraged me
and intensified my hunger to seek Him.

One night I was called out on a pastoral duty to
Dunmurry. There was a traffic hold-up in front of the
King's Hall where thousands were lining up to go in
to hear Elton John the pop singer.

I watched the behaviour of the crowd. Suddenly I
was aware of the presence of the Lord and the Spirit
said: 'Do you think you could fill this place?' I immediately cried: 'No, Lord, but you could!'

Like a flash the thought came back: 'We will fill it
together!'

I thought of what Paul said to the Corinthians: 'He
that is joined to the Lord is one spirit'; and again in 2
Corinthians 6:1: 'We then, as workers together with
Him . . .' I thought of the words in Mark 16:20
concerning the disciples: ' . . . the Lord working with
them, and confirming the word with signs following';
and those of old Judge Gideon in Judges 7:20 when he
shouted: 'The sword of the Lord and of Gideon'.

I went back to my staff the next morning and said:
'Bertie, William, George, Norman, Linda, Shirley –
God wants us to go to the King's Hall and fill it!'

Their response was positive!

'When?'

'How?'

'Let's get on with it!'

That night – Wednesday – I told the Whitewell
people. Their response was beautiful! 'Name the day,
Pastor, and we'll be with you!'

I warned them: 'Remember, no-one is going to help
you. Most people will think we are on an ego-trip

and because of that attitude they will come to the conclusion that we need to be cooled!'

We agreed the theme should be: 'Presenting the King of Kings – the Lord Jesus Christ – in the King's Hall, Belfast'.

I asked every one of my members to bring at least eight persons with them that night.

That was a tall order! But we said it could be done!

Pastor McTernaghan, one of my assistant pastors, who since that first rally has organised every great event in Whitewell, went to the director of the King's Hall, Mr Rees. At first Mr Rees didn't seem to take us seriously. He said: 'Can you fill seven thousand seats?' Their fee for the hire of the hall, £10,000, was mentioned – eventually we brought it down to £5,000 for one night.

That was enough to cool anyone's ardour!

Sunday 31st March 1985 was booked.

We told the Whitewell people that the hire of the hall, the advertising, the free buses, the handbills (450,000 of them), the posters, the beautiful glossy brochure (20,000 of them, distributed free) plus the souvenir hymn book would all cost £20,000. We emphasised we didn't want to ask the public for money after bringing them in to hear the gospel. We set a day aside especially to raise the expenses. When that day came, we raised the £20,000 in *one* offering before we ever got to the King's Hall. We were on our way! During the next two weeks after the Gift Day for the King's Hall, £6,000 came in on top of our tithes and offerings! Every need was met!

We had days of prayer. The prayer times were magnificent. At 6.15 a.m., five hundred people would gather for prayer.

At night, eight hundred people!

The rule of our prayer meetings is: Everyone stands for prayer unless one is ill or elderly. (Abraham, Samuel and Jeremiah stood before the Lord.) This keeps our people alert and each person who prays publicly does so for one minute only. Of course some pray two minutes or three minutes but it's better than boring, meaningless prayers for ten minutes. Sometimes five people would break out into public prayer at once. Now that sounds like confusion, but it's not! Try and picture a large ground floor, packed with 800 people, whoever and wherever they are – be it the front, the sides or the back of the church – praying publicly. The people standing near to them support them with their Amens and Hallelujahs. When it gets going, it is beautiful to behold and the worship is like the sound of many waters!

Our biggest single prayer meeting consisted of one thousand people. If we never got to the King's Hall, it was worth all those prayer meetings: people were in touch with God!

The handbills that were distributed were tremendous. One shipyard man shouted at Norman (my son-in-law) at 7 o'clock one morning: 'I've had four of these handbills already.' Back came the reply: 'If you have five you'll get a free tumbler.' Some days it was hard labour, other days it was sheer fun!

Our young people stuck posters everywhere, much to the annoyance of many people, and our telephones were busy with protesters! I tried to advise our young people – but at the same time, I was proud of them. With young people like this there's a future for Ulster!

At last the 31st March came! The first thing that happened that day was that the church was burgled – three doors were broken, the offices ransacked and some of our stained glass windows were broken. Not a good omen for what we were hoping to have that day.

We cleared up the mess, got on with the morning service, and gave our last minute instructions to the people. They were like an army – an army mobilised, ready for action. I couldn't eat my dinner – I just prayed and walked around the garden and drank cups of tea. I had one telephone call from a pastor – he sounded like Job's comforter! 'I'm sure you're lonely.' (He was right! I didn't need reminding of that!) 'I'll be thinking about you.' And off he went into his own wee world.

At six o'clock I left for the King's Hall. I wanted to be on my own with my thoughts. As I approached the Lisburn Road, noticing the advertisement at Shaftesbury Square for the meeting, the sight that met my eyes would have taken a tear out of a stone. There before me was a cavalcade of buses and cars packed with enthusiastic and eager people.

At 6.30 p.m. the ground floor was packed. At 6.40 p.m. we had to open the gallery. In less than ten minutes it was crammed. Even at the back of the platform where the statue of the old King (George V) stood, people were crowding in.

At 7 p.m. they were still coming! Rows and rows of extra chairs were put out to house all the people. Every nook and cranny of that great historical hall was, as they say in Ulster, 'bunged'!

I was overwhelmed. I could hardly lead the opening hymn. I spluttered, and struggled to fight back the tears, trying to appear composed but that only made things worse. But this was God! God and the Whitewell people had not only filled the King's Hall but packed it to the ceiling.

Mr Rees, the director, stated that on that particular night 8,500 were present. We said that if we had got five to six thousand to attend it would still have been quite an achievement. But eight thousand five hundred – it was! A miracle of God's great power! (After that meeting, the King's Hall authorities said that the crowd limit would be six thousand seats, as a fire precaution.)

And remember, there was no great preacher that night. Billy Graham had preached in the King's Hall,

Principal George Jeffreys, Jack Shuler together with a one thousand voice choir. But this was just a Belfast boy from Spring Street doing the preaching!

As I look back at it all now I feel I could have done much better! But I was overwhelmed, nervous and over-anxious. We have been to the King's Hall seven times since. We are getting used to it. We have also been to Windsor Park, the Northern Ireland national football stadium; the various large leisure centres holding thousands; Inver Park football stadium and Crusaders football stadium.

But we will never forget that first night at the King's Hall. I preached that night on 'Being Ashamed of Christ'. When I asked 'Who would like to come to Christ?' two hundred and fifty persons gave their hearts to the Lord Jesus. And people were healed in their seats without personally being ministered to! During the next two weeks, ministers telephoned me to say that as a result of the rally, they had new faces in their church and new converts, too, who had been saved in the King's Hall. This was the Lord's doing and it was marvellous in our eyes!

13

Windsor Park Football Stadium

The Whitewell people had got a taste of largeness of vision, and would never be the same again.

But we realised we had made a mistake in our preparations for the King's Hall: one night was not enough!

The response was terrific. My home was flooded with letters from people who had appreciated the rally. Also our Church Office received telephone calls from people under conviction of sin from that one night, and wanting to get saved. They were pointed to Christ over the telephone. Even the following night (Monday) our prayer meeting was packed. Five people who had been at the King's Hall twenty-four hours earlier had come to the prayer meeting to get saved! We should have booked the hall, no matter how great the cost, for a long week-end at least!

However, this was a first attempt, and I stressed to myself that God leads His servants and His people step by step. I recalled that at the end of the King's Hall meeting, I had asked the congregation if they would come again if we could book the Hall soon. They had responded with a rapturous wave of applause.

I looked at the calendar – there was time to do something else before the holiday season came upon us.

But Mr Rees informed us that the hall was booked right through to the autumn – the month of October, in fact.

Again I took to the road, seeking the Lord. I believed we could touch the whole land. 'Where can we go, Lord?' Back came the answer: 'Windsor Park'! This was Linfield Football Club's stadium and the ground of the Northern Ireland International Team. I was staggered. Would the people come? Would the White-wellers back me? How would my staff and board react?

The first people I went to were my staff. Their reply was: 'It's a tall order, but we are with you.' I called a Church Meeting and the Whitewellers listened. The theme of my address was 'A Rising Tide lifts all Boats'. Even boats with holes in them! I felt that the first rally was the beginning of the tide, but we needed another one to push the tide to shore. The need of the land consumed me and was eating me up inside. I left the meeting open for comments. One by one those Whitewell people stood to their feet and said: 'If God has told you – we'll go with you!' At once the machinery was put into action. Linfield Football Club agreed. The date was set for 16th June 1985 at 7 p.m. – only two and a half months after the King's Hall. We placed a special announcement in the newspaper and it read as follows: 'As we cannot have the King's Hall for several months we invite the People of Ulster to our Mammoth Rally on Lord's Day, June 16th, 1985 at Windsor Park Football Stadium. There will be seating (under cover) for twelve thousand five hundred people.'

We sat down with the Linfield Football Board and with all facilities opened to us their asking price was £10,000. I bargained until they came down to £8,000. We shook hands – we were on our way!

Immediately 500,000 handbills were ordered, together with 5,000 posters. All the newspapers in the land from the local to the national daily were advertising that the rally would be held in two weeks!

The marvellous Whitewell people were to give me in *one* Sunday another £20,000 to meet all costs!

Six prayer meetings each week were arranged – three at 6.15 a.m. in the morning and three at 8.00 p.m. at night. Doors were rapped, posters were positioned, letters were sent, open-air meetings were held in the city centre for one hour every day for five days, with different people shouting the time and date of the rally. At a later date an aeroplane circled the city carrying a banner with the message: 'Windsor Park – June 16th at 7 p.m.'

But in the middle of all this activity and preparation, news hit the United Kingdom of the Bradford City Football Club's terrible fire disaster, when their wooden stand caught fire and where people perished in the flames.

Almost immediately the Football Association ordered that every grandstand of every stadium should be inspected; thus the South Stand of Linfield Football Club (which held 3,500 people) was declared unsafe and unfit.

We were not unduly troubled as there was still the new stand – the North Stand built from EEC funds – which seated nearly 7,000 people; and the Railway Stand, which held over 3,000.

But imagine our dismay when the telephone rang and Linfield stated that there was a clause in the agreement relating to the new stand saying it could not be used for a political or religious meeting, and that according to the orders of the Irish Football Association no other stand could be used for the rally due to the Bradford fire disaster!

We were devastated – my entire staff cried. We had already spent over £10,000 on handbills, posters, advertising and the hire of the great giant platform. I couldn't speak for an hour – I just sat down with my thoughts. Did God really tell me to go to Windsor Park? I believed He did! The adrenaline began to flow again as I picked myself up.

The telephones started to ring – BBC Television, Ulster Television, all were coming down to see me. I was interviewed, and that night we were on peak viewing time. The *Belfast Telegraph* front page headline read: 'Church slams IFA red tape'.

The next morning the *Newsletter* headline was: 'Rally at soccer pitch offside'. The *Newsletter* read: 'Pastor sticks to Rally plans despite Grandstand shock!' Every day the papers, the radio and television talked about the way we were treated by the IFA and the government.

God was telling me this rally was of Him – He had brought the Whitewell Church and its message to the attention of the nation.

I tried a last minute effort to get the North Stand open. I went to see Dr Paisley who arranged a meeting for me at Stormont with Mr Nicolas Scott, who very kindly and graciously told me that he was powerless to do anything because of the legal clause.

Once again my heart sank down to the depths. No grandstands. No cover. What if it rained?

I called a special meeting of the Whitewell people. I told them everything – the pros and cons. This had to be their decision. Whatever it was, I would abide by it, but I was still convinced that we should go!

They stood up to a man and applauded and cheered. 'We are going to Windsor Park.' I asked: 'What if it rains?' 'Then it rains, but we are going!'

Someone asked: 'If people can't sit in the stands where can they sit?' 'We will hire chairs!' Every day for five days sixty men and women from Whitewell plus the men who were building the great platform and the men and women who were driving our buses fetched and carried literally thousands of chairs to put around the track and on the Spion Kop. I never saw

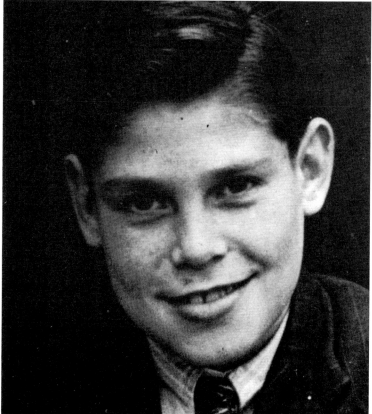

Top: Nettlefield Primary School *Bottom:* Park Parade School

As a young boy, kneeling with his Sunday School teacher, Sammy Jamison, asking Jesus into his heart. Artist: Samuel McCrory

Top: The drawing office at Harland and Wolff *Right:* The old home (14 Spring Street) before demolition

Samuel McCrory's impression of Pastor McConnell praying on a hillside overlooking the City of Belfast

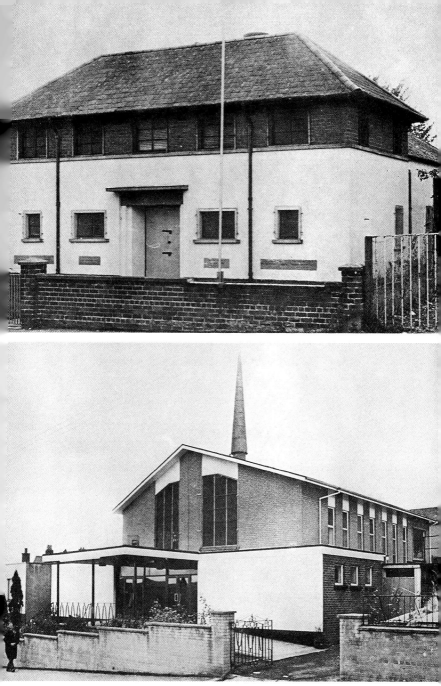

Top: Where it all began *Bottom:* The second phase

Above: Windsor Park Football Stadium – Sunday 16th June, 1985
Below: The King's Hall Rally – Sunday 31st March, 1985

Dr and Mrs James
McConnell on the occasion
of the conferment of
Divinity Degree –
19th July, 1986

A typical Sunday night rally at Whitewell. Samuel McCrory

work and dedication like it. We put our last advertisement in the papers 'Ulster people to solve Ulster's problems. It's on – presenting the champion of champions – the Lord Jesus Christ.'

There's something of a personal nature I would now write and I leave the Godly man and the Spiritual woman to judge.

The Tuesday before we went to Windsor Park, I went to bed late after having a time of prayer. About four-thirty in the morning, I woke up soaking with perspiration and found myself shouting and waking the whole house!

I suppose one could say that was natural, it was a nightmare after all the stress and tension of the IFA's closure of the grandstands and the hassle of dealing with all the red tape!

But here's what really happened: I dreamed I was standing in the middle of the ground. I was shouting to the people, 'Christ loves you, there's nothing that He cannot do for you.' And I remember particularly saying to them: 'Look at how He took the trouble to go through Samaria to find the woman at a well and change her life. He can do that for you, and He can do that for this land!'

At this juncture a dark figure towered above me and said: 'This land belongs to me, I'll never let you have it.' I felt my shoulders grabbed by his two powerful hands.

The dream was so vivid I actually felt pain go right through my body draining me of every ounce of strength I had. 'Who are you?' I asked, and I woke up hearing a voice in the dark faintly saying: 'I am the Prince of this Land!'

Now whatever conclusions you may come to, that experience was vivid and was real to me.

When my friend and colleague Bertie Blake called for me the next morning, he found me totally drained. I turned to the Book of Daniel, chapter 10, to read of how Daniel set his heart to seek God for twenty-one days eating no pleasant bread. As the anointing of the Holy Spirit came upon him, he saw in his vision the angel of God's presence coming in to him. But verses 12 and 13 revealed to Daniel and to us what is going on in the heavenlies. The angel of God said:

> Fear not, Daniel: for from the first day that thou didst set thine heart to understand, and to chasten thyself before thy God, thy words were heard, and I am come for thy words. But the prince of the kingdom of Persia withstood me one and twenty days: but, lo, Michael, one of the chief princes, came to help me; and I remained there with the kings of Persia.

Now let your eye go to verse 20. The angel of God continued to speak to Daniel and he said: 'Knowest thou wherefore I come unto thee? And now will I return to fight with the prince of Persia and when I am gone forth, lo, the prince of Grecia shall come.'

What does this strange language mean? Who was this prince of Persia who withstood the mighty angel of God? It wasn't the human prince of Persia, it was the spiritual prince of Persia – the prince that ruled Persia was a Prince of Darkness! I am convinced this Ulster of ours and the United Kingdom are held in the grasp of the Prince of Darkness, and until God's blood-washed people get together in unity and love and set their hearts to seek God like Daniel, that grip of this Demon Prince will tighten and intensify. Remember what Jesus said in Matthew 17:21 when the disciples asked Him why they couldn't deliver the boy from the unclean and lunatic spirit. 'Because of your unbelief ... Howbeit this kind goeth not out but by prayer and fasting.'

I realised the Windsor Park Rally was out of my league. I was dealing with the power of darkness. When I read Ephesians 6:12, I see that the apostle

Paul agrees. He says we have to 'put on the whole armour of God'. Why? 'For we wrestle not against flesh and blood, but against principalities, against powers, against the rulers of the darkness of this world, against spiritual wickedness in high places'.

Never forget this – if you set your heart to seek God, to walk with God, to please God, to serve God, to extend the Kingdom of God, Satan will show himself.

Sunday morning, 16th June, came. The day was dull and cloudy with a cool breeze, but spirits were high.

The BBC was there. The newspaper reporters were there. And the people came.

As they were coming, the reporters asked, 'How many do you think are here?' 'I don't know', I replied, 'but it looks good!' At that moment, the people broke into the Railway Stand, and it was packed! The chairs around the ground and Spion Kop were all full. As I looked up at the South Stand, I saw that approximately 200 people had climbed into there, too!

At this juncture, let the *Belfast Newsletter* tell the story. The headlines on Monday morning stated: 'Pastor's sermon is heard by thousands. Hands unite across the divide'.

The goals of faith and hope united Protestants and Roman Catholics in the unlikely surroundings of Windsor Park last night . . . The home of Northern Ireland's football played host to more than 12,000 people who came together for a gospel rally at the famous ground.

The report covered a full page, giving photographs of the crowd and those who took part. At night the *Belfast Telegraph* gave similar coverage, as did television.

Christ was glorified! Another 200 precious souls had come to the Saviour. But what thrilled me was that people had travelled to the stadium as far as from Crossmaglen, Dundalk, Newry and Dublin, and that many Roman Catholics, hearing of Christ's finished work on Calvary, asked Him into their hearts.

Once again, as with the first rally, for the next three days the telephones rang in the office and in my home, Men and women who had been at Windsor Park were still under conviction of their need, and wanting to be saved! They were dealt with and helped.

Looking back at it all now, I think that the Windsor Park Rally was very significant in the mind of the Holy Spirit. While he told me to go, he also knew the end from the beginning and knew the difficulties that would face me.

But during those three weeks of intense preparation and conflict regarding the grandstands, the Holy Spirit was showing the people of our province that there was a group of believers who loved the Lord Jesus and in spite of the obstacles thrown in their way were determined to serve Him. It's important for a country to know there's a people within it whose yea is yea and whose nay is nay and who carry out what they say even if it costs them!

Christ was glorified and people's lives were changed – both Protestant and Catholic.

After the Windsor Park Rally there was a period of respite because it was the holidays and the people were tired. For the next three months, people were coming and going – but God was still at work in Whitewell. The church continued to be packed and without fail, souls were being saved every week at every meeting. But God was to do more great things as we shall read later on.

The holidays passed and people were beginning to settle down again, coming back refreshed. I had felt restrained of the Holy Spirit not to take any holidays, and not to accept any of the preaching engagements that came regularly from the United States and Canada. My heart was so burdened for the province – I didn't want to leave it. Of course this may sound silly but that's how I really felt – I wanted to show the Lord Jesus I was available for any task He might ask me to do.

I met my staff again and my brethren and we decided that it was time to go back to the King's Hall again. But this time we would go for *two* nights – Saturday and Sunday.

I was pleased at the response from my staff – it was they who were encouraging me to take the two nights in a row. What would be the theme of the two meetings?

We decided the theme would be: 'If Christ can heal an individual – He can heal a land.'

I wrote a letter to the two leading newspapers of our province asking Christians to support these two meetings. The Whitewell people – what a marvellous crowd – once again went forward to the task of rapping doors, distributing leaflets, posters, etc.; giving me on one Sunday to meet the financial commitments another £20,000. On top of all their tithes and offerings and missionary pledges they gave me over £80,000 to meet what we called 'The home mission front'!) At the end of the financial year, counting tithes, offerings, missionary commitments, love gifts, etc., the total church income amounted to £500,000.) However, I sensed they were tired; but I noticed they were tired *in* the work but not *of* the work!

At this time, I was particularly burdened for them. I wanted with all my heart to see them encouraged for the work they were doing.

The dates of the two meetings were Saturday 5th October and Sunday 6th October. We advertised the Saturday meeting as an 'Inspiration Meeting' for Christians. We wondered if many would come. Again, we had no churches or ministers whatever supporting us; it seemed they were locked in their own wee world! Anyway, Saturday night was a kind of a night when everyone stayed at home.

To our delight, over 5,000 people came and filled the ground floor. It was a glorious night – a night of singing and worship. I preached on the subject of: 'The Middle Wall of Partition'. It was a real believers' meeting – but fifty persons came to Christ. I felt we were slowly but surely breaking down the prejudice among God's people. We showed them we loved and wanted them and that we wanted them to love us!

The next night again would be another great hurdle. Many of the believers who were with us on the Saturday night would be in their own churches. But to our pleasure, 5,500 people turned up for the Sunday night rally. My subject: 'When God Abandons a Nation – a Church – an Individual'.

Over 200 people came out for Christ. It was tremendous!

That weekend 250 people were caught in Christ's net!

The Master had encouraged the Whitewell people and I was so pleased for them. Counting the morning service in our local church, 13,000 people had heard God's word that weekend.

Many people in Ulster were sitting up and taking notice – even the politicians on both sides of the political divide. But we made it absolutely clear – we were not interested in politics nor in its drama and intrigue. God had called me to be a pastor and to stand in the middle of the religious and political divide with the precious gospel of God's son, the Lord Jesus Christ.

If Ulster could be unified it would not be through the politicians nor the political parties but through the gospel! I remember being at a church conference where they were discussing how the country could be healed and how the IRA and UVF could be stopped. One brother, looked upon as a kind of an oddity, said: 'Get them all saved!' The members of the conference laughed! But I went home thinking seriously about his statement.

The man was right. If I could get Protestant and Roman Catholic saved then I felt I must stay out of politics. This is not to say I don't have my political opinions, for I feel Ulster is part of the United Kingdom and I want Ulster to stay part of the United Kingdom. When the opportunity comes I use my democratic right and vote for the same. But in the words of old Alexander Whyte of Free St Georges, 'I aim to keep my seed or gospel basket clean'!

Regarding the Anglo-Irish Agreement, I believe it is totally undemocratic, pushing the majority of Ulster people into a situation they do not desire nor want. Time after time, in no uncertain manner, they have demonstrated in every election their desire to stay in the United Kingdom.

I and my staff were with the thousands who stood around the City Hall to make our protest in a Christian manner; but we are not to be associated with a faction who protest with violence, intimidation and fear. But that is as far as it goes! The gospel is my life, my heart, my soul, my career, my future, my eternity; and the only way that Catholic and Protestant can be united is through that gospel of the finished work of the Lord Jesus!

Many times in these rallies and in my church – much to the annoyance of many – I stress there may be partition in this country, but there is no partition in Hell! If a Protestant dies without accepting the finished work of the Lord Jesus on Calvary and if a Catholic dies without accepting the finished work of the Lord Jesus on Calvary – both of them will meet in the same Hell!

If a Catholic accepts the finished work of Christ on Calvary and a Protestant does exactly the same – both will meet in the same Heaven – saved through Jesus' Blood!

What troubles and annoys me is the hypocrisy of many so-called Evangelical Christians in Ulster.

When they hear of Roman Catholics being saved in Whitewell they retort: 'But have they come out of the Roman Church?' The answer is 'Yes' and a total 'Yes'! Yet none of us have ever told them to do so. How do they know to come out? You see, I believe it is the way you should present the gospel. The gospel has always been a gospel of separation and if the gospel is preached properly in the power of the Holy Spirit that Holy Spirit who is showing them their need of Christ, will also show them that salvation is not in a church nor a creed nor a priest but totally in God's lovely sinless Son, the Lord Jesus Christ.

We have found that when a precious Catholic (after coming to Christ) asks for baptism by total immersion in water and sits down at the Lord's Table to remember the Lord's death, that Catholic has come out of the Catholic Church!

Let me tell you of a remarkable incident in the life of one of our Catholic members. He had given his life to Christ on a Sunday. Five days later he went to confession as usual, gave his personal testimony to the priest – how he had found Christ – then gently and kindly told the priest he would never be back again to confession or the mass, for the Lord Jesus had forgiven him of all his sins. No one told him to do this. I don't think I would have had the courage to tell him to do so! But Christ had got a hold of him and he had got a hold of Christ and that was the inevitable outcome.

Another Catholic lady came in under conviction to Whitewell and went to her parish priest telling him how she felt. In her own words, he couldn't do anything for her. She came back to Whitewell, got saved, and has become a faithful member of the church.

This has happened to scores of Roman Catholics who have got saved and become members of our church.

But here's a poser for Protestants: Have you come out of your denomination?

'What do you mean, James McConnell?'

I'll tell you what I mean; there are scores of Presbyterian, Church of Ireland and Methodist ministers who don't preach the gospel, who are modernistic, who are ecumenical and who doubt the authority of the Scriptures. Should I encourage precious souls who have come to Christ during our gospel meetings to go back to their denomination? My answer: 'No way!'

The first thing I ask when they propose to go back to their church is this: 'Is your minister saved? For instance, what you heard tonight and believed tonight, does he preach that?' If the answer is no, I encourage them to stay with us for a while until they find their feet. Should they so desire, God can lead them elsewhere to find a true and real spiritual home of their own, where the minister is a born-again Christian who faithfully preaches the new birth and teaches believers how to walk.

You may think my language strong; but listen to this language taken from Paul's letter to Timothy. In II Timothy 3:5, Paul talks about formalism, modernism. Then he goes on to say regarding these pedlars in God's work: ' . . . having a form of godliness, but denying the power thereof: from such turn away'. That language is clear-cut, hiding nothing and giving undoubted direction.

The need of Northern Ireland constantly and daily troubles me, troubles me in this sense: there are so many preachers of the gospel, there are so many churches, there are so many born-again Christians and yet our land is not improving. What is wrong? Because our Lord puts it powerfully in Matthew's Gospel chapter 5 that the child of God is 'salt', a kind of antiseptic, a stayer of decay, a halter of decomposition to stem the rottenness in society.

Also He said that the child of God is a 'light', shining in the darkness of evil and corruption, showing the way to peace and to God.

So what's wrong with this province? Preachers, like politicians, are ten a penny. Open a packet of tea and you will find a preacher in it! Open any 'Heinz 57 Variety' product and you will find a preacher there also! Go home, and hiding behind the bushes of your garden you will find a preacher. There are so many of them and yet our Lord said: 'The harvest truly is great and the labourers are few; pray ye that the Lord of the harvest will send forth labourers into His harvest.'

I think the question we have to ask is: What sort of labourers are in the harvest field of Northern Ireland? We need effective labourers! According to Revelation chapters 1 and 2 those seven churches of Asia were candlesticks, lampstands – shining, giving light. If that is the case, were every blood-washed, spirit-filled church in Northern Ireland a real candlestick, a real lampstand, then this country should be full of light, and revive and come back to God.

But what sort of labourers are James McConnell and his staff? And what sort of church is Whitewell? Are they a true lampstand, a real candlestick? I think one of the reasons the blessing of God is upon us is because we realise at all costs we must shine and we must sting like salt!

There must be a constant searching of our hearts! There must be, often, a self-examination and a cry for cleansing, so that the Holy Spirit can anoint us! If He doesn't – then our lives and our ministries are ineffective and useless. So, then, will our Church and churches be also!

14

The week at Whitewell

At this stage, let me give you some insight of the average working week at Whitewell.

My office staff commence their morning at 9.00 a.m., working through until 4.00 p.m. My pastors, Robert Blake, William McTernaghan and Norman Hobson, together with two of my Elders, Charles Purse and Alec Brown, report also at the office at the same time and work until they are tired!

Usually we begin the day with a word of prayer and a cup of tea then we discuss those who would need our immediate attention that day!

My office staff consists of two secretaries. My daughter, Linda Hobson, looks after all the financial operations of the church – which are quite considerable. Linda also sings in the group Dayspring, which is making an impact in the Evangelical musical world. Shirley Skilling, who is responsible for typing all my publishing material, attends to my correspondence and keeps me right regarding appointments, etc. Shirley is also the leader of the fabulous Whitewell Temple Choir.

My full-time staff are very dedicated and loyal people who think nothing of working long hours at any time of day or night – I would be lost without them!

We have a full-time caretaker, Norman Graham,

who is marvellous, ably assisted by Thomas Braiden
(affectionately known as 'Captain Braiden') and Mrs
Sadie McDowell, who together keep the great Sanctuary spotless and beautiful (and that is quite a job!).

Monday is the day we make our report, and after all
the Sunday services, etc., we usually arrive exhausted!

We have a pre-school playgroup from Monday to
Friday (9.30 a.m. until 12.30 p.m.) with an attendance
of twenty-four children, both Protestant and Catholic.
Also on Monday night we have our usual prayer
meeting numbering about 800 people.

On Tuesday morning we have another prayer
meeting from 10.00 a.m. to 11.00 a.m. for those who
are on shift work and for others who want another
time with God. This morning prayer meeting is very
popular. Then on Tuesday night in both our church
buildings and also in a rented school, we have the
Girls' Brigade and Boy Scouts. Counting both
companies, we have well over 250 members, with a
tremendous group of born-again and dedicated officers
– male and female.

On Wednesday night at 8.00 p.m. we hold our
weekly Bible study with attendances in the region of
800 again. Often when the pastor has a special subject
the crowd can swell to one thousand!

On Thursday, our youth organisations are in operation again. Also, the Whitewell Temple Choir hold
their weekly choir practice.

Friday morning, the Mother and Toddlers Group
meet; then at night the Youth Choir hold their practice
and the Youth Fellowship meet in the old church
building from 10.00 p.m. to midnight for prayer.

This brings us to Saturday, when from 9.30 a.m. to
12 noon we hold our great Bible School, which has
proved a great blessing to many. The Bible School is
under the direction of Pastor Eric Briggs from
Armagh. Two hundred students attend this school
faithfully every week. Usually every Saturday, there

is a wedding – sometimes two! And on Saturday night from 7.30 p.m. to 10.30 p.m. we have our Youth Fellowship with ages ranging from fifteen to thirty. This club is packed and is under the leadership of Pastor Norman Hobson.

Every day, from 9.00 a.m. to 4.00 p.m., our church garage is in operation keeping the 'Whitewell Wheels' rolling! We have six men on the staff working night and day making sure all the buses are in working order for the people and for the youth organisations. The buses never cool – we have thirty-five of them and these brethren faithfully maintain and repair them. It is exhausting work, especially in the winter when it is cold and wet, as they are often called out in the middle of the night to repair one that has broken down or to tow one back to base.

The men who drive our buses are worth their weight in gold. They do this voluntarily – in fact, some of them never get a proper meal on Sunday until they are home, late on Sunday night. We usually have two drivers to each bus so that our brethren can get a break occasionally. I call them our mini-pastors, for they let us know who is missing and who may be having problems.

As I said, the Lord's Day in Whitewell is a 'High Day' and the people love it! Our morning service begins at 11.00 a.m. and it is strictly a believers' service where the service is centred around the Lord's Table. The church family gather (an average of 1,300 people) to hear God's word and break bread. At the same time, two nurseries are in operation – one for the many babies in Whitewell (for 75% of our members are young people), and another downstairs for the three to five age group. This helps families to worship God together and to enjoy the service.

In the afternoon at 3.00 p.m., nine Sunday Schools (in the various areas around the country) take place. What a tremendous work that is and what a marvellous bunch of teachers! There is also an adult Bible Class, taken by Charles Purse and David Cairns. Incidentally, David is the editor of our Church Magazine *The Standard of Truth*. At night, from 6.45 p.m. to 8.45 p.m. we have our great evangelistic service. The attendances range from 1,500 to 1,600 people, the church being packed to capacity with people sitting everywhere. Again the two nurseries are in operation.

The Whitewell choirs and groups minister each week in song. We have three choirs, the Children's Choir (numbering up to 100), the Whitewell Youth Choir (70 members) and the Whitewell Temple Choir (100 members). Also, we have a group called 'Lightshine' (they number about seven) and a young people's rock group who are talented and who take many services around the country, but who make a point of staying in their local church on Lord's Day. Their name is 'Noah's Ark', they number about six – and they have won many young people to Christ! Lastly, we have 'Dayspring', who are extremely talented, and who are now writing their own material. They have taken many concerts, have sung before some of the greatest audiences in the United Kingdom and are constantly swamped with bookings!

The loyalty and faithfulness of all our choirs and groups is second to none. They are very much local church orientated, and while they are popular and are asked to take many services and functions, they insist on being in their own local church on Lord's Day. Whitewell is a big family and we intend to stay a family!

For the past ten years we have had a weekly 'Church Bulletin'. This Bulletin informs the people in Whitewell, and indeed those outside, of what is going on and of our future plans.

On Tuesday and Friday nights – rain, hail or snow – we have four teams of 'door to door' workers, who rap doors, personally witness, distribute literature and

extend a hearty invitation to Whitewell. Indeed many
people have been led to Christ through this ministry.
The workers meet one night a week to pray for their
labours in this particular ministry.

So a week at Whitewell is a week of tremendous,
exhausting activity. Then, if there is a Special Rally,
there will be extra prayer meetings from 6.15 a.m. to
7.30 a.m. and 10.00 a.m. to 11.00 a.m., or a big Friday
night meeting from 8.00 p.m. to 9.30 p.m. Again, the
people faithfully attend!

On top of all this, homes are pastorally visited, as
are hospitals and prisons – you name it, we are there!

There is also a small group of ladies called the 'Care
Group' who go around those in need (both young and
old) offering help and assistance.

When we are giving the church announcements we
laughingly say, 'If you get to all these meetings, you
won't even have time to backslide'.

Another aspect of our work is the tape ministry
which has become an institution in Whitewell and
which under the direction of Jim Thompson and Albert
Beattie has been a blessing to literally hundreds of
people. God in His grace has set men in set places.
Jim Thompson came into the Whitewell church ten
years ago – deep in sin. Jim was a vagrant for many
years, wandering about aimlessly with no direction in
life, and Christ got the hold of him and made him a
trophy of His grace. Jim Thompson's story has been
repeated in scores of key men and key women who
make up the ministry of the Whitewell church. These
tapes are heard all over the world and we have many
gracious letters in our files from people who have come
to Christ through the Whitewell tapes. One popular
tape that has sold thousands is: 'Songs they sing at
Whitewell'. Jim Thompson very ably has culled all the
anointed hymns and choruses the great congregation
sing at Whitewell. Also at every service our two
faithful sound men, William Marshall and David

Ramsay, are present, looking after every one who takes part.

We also have a bookshop run by Mr and Mrs C. Purse, where many people get spiritual help; and a shop organised by what we call 'the Rathcoole Gang', Betty Eaton and her friends – what a remarkable group of women! To help our missionary outreach, we have a Missionary Board who meet once a month. This board is composed of ten members. Then we have our Iron Curtain Outreach supervised by Cecil Johnston, and our Home Mission Outreach for which John Armstrong is responsible. All this goes on every week at Whitewell.

I remember Pastor Blake saying: 'When one is away from Whitewell for a week, they feel they are missing something.' This feeling is endorsed by many people!

15

The arrow of the Lord's deliverance

For the next five months – the end of 1985 and the beginning of 1986 – we began to settle again into assembly life, dealing with new converts, counselling and visiting all types of homes and people, trying to make our local church strong.

I endeavoured by the help of the Holy Spirit to make every service interesting, challenging and instructive. Every week without fail, men and women were coming to Christ, as they still are today.

But I was praying for, preaching for and crying for a committed people. The only drawback about a big church is that there are many 'hangers on' – people who come to you but who are not committed to any church. They claim to be saved all right, but they won't give their allegiance to any leader of any assembly. Should there arise a crisis in the church or should the church pass through a brief time of routine, you will see them drifting off somewhere else, and when they hear of an upsurge of blessing, back they come again!

You get others who are quite content to come, say, on a Sunday morning or a Sunday night – they want you and they don't want you. They want you to want them and yet they don't want you to want them! Every

church has them, they are the breakings of many a
servant of God's heart. They come when it suits them.
They give when it suits them. You see, they are not
committed. If they were totally committed to Christ,
He would lead them, guide them and instruct them.
And so they come, and fill many a seat you wish good
people with dedication and commitment would occupy.

So I began to preach strongly about commitment,
dedication, holiness, living right, being real – in order
that I could win some of them (that is, if they had
anything of God in them).

I went back to making three new sermons or messages each week, plus two prayer meetings. My hours
of work were literally from morning to night – trying
to give God's people the finest of the wheat.

I noticed when I put the pressure on, they (the
hangers on) were conspicuous by their absence. I
believed with all my heart, God was searching and
looking for a people for His name and I kept telling
the Whitewell people this.

One night, during the very early hours of the
morning, I was reading for my private devotion II
Kings 13:14 – 25. It was about the death of that
wonderful man of God, Elisha, the man with the
double portion of Elijah's anointing. Joash the King
of Israel came down to his death-bed and wept over
the old prophet's face crying: 'My father, my father,
the chariot of Israel, and the horsemen thereof.'

I particularly noted that fifty years earlier when
Elijah (in II Kings 2:12) was taken up into heaven in
a chariot of fire, young Elisha, crying at the departure
of the old prophet, said the very same thing – 'My
father, my father, the chariot of Israel, and the
horsemen thereof.' What did Elisha and Joash mean?

Surely they meant the nation's true defence and
deterrent lay not in horses and chariots and armour,
but in real men of God, living among them with the
presence of God in their lives, manifesting their spiri-

tual leadership in their Godly lives, their prophetic spirit.

I read on. In verse 15, the old prophet said to Joash: 'Take bow and arrows.' He continued, 'Put thine hand upon the bow', and Joash put his hand to the bow, 'and Elisha put his hands upon the king's hands'.

The next command was in verse 17: 'Open the window eastward'. Then Elisha said, 'Shoot', and he shot!

Then Elisha said: 'The arrow of the Lord's deliverance, and the arrow of deliverance from Syria: for thou shalt smite the Syrians in Aphek, till thou have consumed them.'

As I read this, I began to realise the Holy Spirit was showing me something very important. Elisha spoke to Joash again (verse 18): 'Take the arrows . . . Smite upon the ground.' Joash smote three times and stopped.

At this, Elisha, the old man of God, was angry with him and scolded: 'Thou shouldest have smitten five or six times; if so, Syria would be utterly consumed: whereas now thou shalt smite Syria – but thrice.' Elisha meant that Joash would not have a complete victory, but Syria would only be subdued.

I asked, 'Lord, what will thou have me to do?'

The Spirit replied: 'Are you willing to strike and strike and strike and strike again and again and again – until this land knows my power and presence?'

I was deeply challenged, convicted and stirred. I began to recollect each great rally and the burden of those big meetings. The stress, the strain, the labour of those meetings to reach precious souls. I was frightened to overtax the sheep in Whitewell and exhaust them. But was I not preaching constantly on commitment? I said: 'Lord, give me good men and women in Whitewell – young, old and middle-aged.'

I went to the Whitewell people again. With fresh vigour they gave themselves to the task of filling the

King's Hall – four nights in a row! Sunday, Monday, Tuesday and Wednesday. It was the month of June – the World Cup was on, but God in His grace and goodness did not let us down, the money was given and the bills were met! The smallest attendance of the four great rallies was on a Monday night when 4,000 turned up! From Sunday to Wednesday, counting the morning service, 18,000 heard the word of God. Three hundred people came to Christ, plus scores of backsliders.

The thrill of those meetings was that many pastors telephoned me the following weekend telling of people attending their church who were saved in the King's Hall!

The holidays came. From the end of June to September, I went back to my pastoral activities with my faithful staff of full-time workers. But the word I was given was – 'Strike again!'

However, in the month of May – just before the King's Hall Rally – working with the local Elim Church in the town of Larne, we went to the Regal Cinema where 800 people crowded in to hear the gospel with more precious souls being saved.

This little event encouraged us for a much bigger one and in spite of the holiday period, we went to the Larne Football Club and booked their little stadium for another great rally.

The Whitewellers went to the task with great enthusiasm, and Friday, 22nd August at 7.30 p.m. was the date and time set aside. It rained for three full days; on the day of the rally, the rain pelted down. We didn't know what to do. At 5.30 p.m. – two hours before the meeting – the rain stopped! We set up the platform in record-breaking time – the rally was on!

3,000 people packed the little stadium – people were standing in their hundreds on the roads listening! Fifty-five persons came to Christ.

The *Belfast Telegraph* came down to the rally, giving

a full page report on the meeting which was read by scores of thousands.

Little did I know this was the start of a series of 'smites' (the word according to Elijah) right through the country. The Holy Spirit was leading us step by step and increasing our faith.

Soon we were to hire the great Leisure Centre (seating 2,000 people) on the famous Shankill Road, Belfast, for two nights in September. The place was packed and scores of souls came to Christ.

That particular week, while preparing for those two meetings, my life was threatened by telephone and by letter. Satan was being stirred up!

But I realised that what we were doing was comparatively safe.

DERRY

Now, what about the Catholic section of the country? Of course we argued that precious Roman Catholics had come to Christ at all our rallies. But they had come to us, we had not gone to them. It was time for us to go to them! The city the Holy Spirit whispered in our hearts was – 'Londonderry' (Derry)!

Someone pointed out that that city was the grave-yard of many a Special Gospel effort. I said: 'We are going!'

Once again, I met the Whitewell people, who said: 'We are going with you!'

We booked the Guild Hall for two nights. We spent three weeks walking the streets of Londonderry – but the hour was coming when we had to walk through the famous Bogside and the Creggan Estates – totally Roman Catholic.

I remember sixty of our brethren marching through those tense estates giving a handbill here and an invitation there! I also recall when we entered the Bogside reading the slogan: 'You are now entering Free Derry'.

But, bless their hearts, there was nothing free about them, they were still bound in sin and deluded by the Prince of Darkness. Meanwhile in the city, about seventy of the sisters of our church swamped the place with leaflets and love! I must say in all honesty and fairness, I was treated worse in other areas. The people of the Bogside and the Creggan (while they did not agree with us) received us kindly and graciously.

One incident stands out during that time: one of our brethren got lost and found himself confronted by a gunman in one of the houses that he was leafletting. He was taken and locked in a coal house for one hour. We thank God he lived to tell the tale!

It was a hard work and at times we were under pressure. But we felt we must make an inroad into the Catholic areas for the Kingdom of God. Five days before the two rallies took place, a sinister incident occurred. I received a telephone call telling me that stuck over all our posters in the city was the word 'Cancelled'. It was a brilliant and skilful attempt to wreck our plans without openly condemning our meetings in the Guild Hall.

I immediately saw this was the work of Satan. I called my pastors and some of my brethren and for the second time that day, we motored down to Londonderry, armed with fresh posters and buckets of paste!

Scores and gangs of youths followed us, watching us as we climbed the walls where the 'Cancelled' posters were, and replaced them. They laughed at us, taunted us, but they didn't harm us! We arrived home at three o'clock in the morning. Wednesday and Thursday – the nights of the meetings – came. One resident of the city said it was over thirty years since he had seen the Guild Hall so packed for a gospel meeting. Over 1,000 people jammed the Guild Hall with people who couldn't get seats standing everywhere. A total of thirty-five people gave their hearts to Christ. Twenty of them were Catholic and fifteen of them were Protestants.

Little did we know what the outcome of those meetings and those days in Londonderry would be. God brought us into contact with a very special young man whose name was John Scott. We asked him to contact those who had given their hearts to Christ and as we had fellowship together, we found a common bond of love and trust which remains to this day. As a result, Whitewell and the group of people he pastored were 'married' (joined together) and it is lovely to see that 'lighthouse' of a church in the city of Derry shining for Jesus. The church is made up of Protestants and Catholics who love one another and who love the Lord Jesus. Whitewell would have an extension in that very important city through God's servant – John Scott.

We were thrilled and encouraged at what God was doing. But Elisha's scolding to Joash was still ringing in my ears – 'You should have smitten until Syria was consumed'.

Where would I strike again?

NEWRY

Now listen to this story. It was Solomon in fact who said in Ecclesiastes 11:1: 'Cast thy bread upon the waters: for thou shalt find it after many days.' Three years earlier, I remember arriving home, when it was brought to my attention that a man was looking for me. I didn't know who he was, but he came back and rapped my door. I found he was a traveller/salesman who had passed by our church many times whilst on the M2 motorway on his way to do business. One day as he passed by our building again, the Spirit of God grabbed him, he had to turn and make his peace with God. He entered the church – all the pastors were out on call, but my caretaker prayed with him and led him to Christ. The man would not go home until he saw me, and when we came together I was able to encourage him more and pray with him. The man was from the town of Newry – 80% Roman Catholic – and his name was John Magowan. Little did I know that day that I was casting my bread upon the waters and I would find it after many days. This man then procured some of our tapes – recordings of the Whitewell services – and passed them on to other people in the town.

I recall one Sunday night, two years ago, three men came from Newry. Two of them, Roman Catholics, gave their lives to Christ. Month by month it became evident that in that town ravaged by violence, burning and bombing there were many hungry hearts yearning after God and His presence. More men were coming from Newry – in particular a young man, John Kernaghan, who had immediately caught and was fired by the Whitewell vision to reach this land of ours for Christ.

The time came when we realised we must again 'smite' or strike out again for God. We visited the town, walked around it and tried to capture its spirit, speaking to the people. I found them, like many other people in Northern Ireland, and for that matter in the world, needy, helpless, longing and searching. We booked the Town Hall for two nights in December 1986. By the way, the two dates we suggested to the manager were the only two vacant nights he had! The place was booked through to the new year.

Once again the machinery of God's people began to roll! Every day, packed buses of our people went down to the town, rapping doors, speaking kindly to people and giving invitations to all and sundry. We wanted to win souls to Christ and we were conscious we were in the enemy's territory. But we wanted to establish a work which C. T. Studd called 'running a rescue shop within a yard of Hell'.

During those weeks, the weather was not pleasant

and many a person opened the door to us (looking at us in amazement) to take a handbill, while the water literally ran off us – we were soaked to the skin! But we loved every minute of it – we were doing it as unto the Lord and there was expectation in our hearts that God would do something.

The night of the first meeting, it snowed. The Whitewellers came in buses and the Town Hall was packed from top to bottom! Our deacons estimated that approximately 250 visitors had come to the meeting in addition to the crowd already there. We were thrilled at the response.

The place was filled with a mixture of Protestants and Catholics. I preached on Romans 10:9, repeatedly saying: 'Salvation is not in a church, a creed, an organisation, but a person – the Lord Jesus Christ.'

The attention was terrific but one could feel the tension – these people had come to 'look me over'! The next night, I preached to a packed house on the subject: 'Who is my Priest?' Speaking lovingly, gently, knowing again the audience was mixed, I exalted the Lord Jesus as the believer's surety, as the believer's only Priest, as the believer's only source of forgiveness. In the two meetings, thirty persons came to Christ – the majority of them, Catholic!

We then announced a weekly Bible Study would be held every Thursday night for those who were interested in learning the Scriptures and getting to know the Lord Jesus better. That weekly Bible Study has emerged into a church and by the time you read this book, a full gospel church will have been planted in Newry, made up of Protestants and Catholics – half of each. The sweetness and unity of that church is beautiful and the times of worship are inspiring.

One of our best young men, David Purse (whose father was shot by the IRA), is now pastoring this church with great love and enthusiasm. We know that

God is going to establish something strong and special in that town.

SPAIN—SCOTLAND—WALES

The Whitewell story has gone on into Spain where we mother four churches ably led by Leslie and Brenda Lyons. Their dedication is an example to any person wishing to enter the ministry. Leslie Lyons is one of the most effective modern-day missionaries working in Spain.

In Falkirk, Scotland, a group of people heard the Whitewell tapes. Pastor Bertie Blake and myself travelled over each fortnight for one year by ferry and car, until the work grew. Then Pastor George McKim, an important member of my staff, went to lead that small assembly. Since then it has grown from strength to strength and plans are underway to build a Sanctuary to house the people.

Whitewell's arm has also gone into South Wales, to the town of Aberdare where approximately fifteen people asked if we could come and help. God supplied them with a man, John Houston, who went over against great odds. Today, John Houston has emerged as a great Christian leader and the little building has become too small for the growth they have experienced.

The Whitewell people affectionately call our young men and their wives who have gone out to pastor these churches 'the branches who have gone over the wall', quoting Jacob's prophecy over Joseph in Genesis 49:22: 'Joseph is a fruitful bough, even a fruitful bough by a well; whose branches run over the wall.'

We predict by the Holy Spirit, all over the United Kingdom in strategic places, the Head of the Church, the Lord Jesus, will open other doors of effectual ministry.

THE METROPOLITAN CHURCH

The question that has been asked of me is whether I and Whitewell intend to start another denomination. My reply to that is definitely No! The Whitewell Church has come into association with a Pentecostal denomination, the Elim Church, and we are thoroughly enjoying precious fellowship with those brethren and look forward to enjoying continually the fellowship of the Elim brethren and churches. We have joined Elim Church Incorporated and wholeheartedly endorse all their guiding principles and aims. But we are not interested in forming a denomination. We are basically a mother church – we like to care for and mother small groups until they grow into strength. Then we go on to some other group which needs our help. We would like to be known, if it is possible, as a movement which from time to time will be anointed of the Spirit of God and led to go to a certain place to bring obvious results as an evidence of being led! This is one of the reasons why we changed our name and officially called our local fellowship 'The Metropolitan Church Whitewell'. The name 'Metropolitan' was used in fond remembrance of Charles Haddon Spurgeon's Tabernacle, London, and his preaching on the doctrines of grace. These doctrines have been fundamental to the growth and blessing of Whitewell. Also, this word 'Metropolitan' which has the root meaning 'mother' encourages us to call our assembly by this name, for at this moment, Whitewell is 'mothering' ten churches.

At this point, the question may be posed: 'What is the difference between an organisation and a movement?' I think there is a slight distinction but the narrow margin makes all the difference! Chambers Dictionary defines the word 'ORGANISATION' as 'the act of organising, to form several parts into an organised "whole" – to arrange'. In other words, to set up

separate parts into a structure! But Chambers
Dictionary defines 'MOVEMENT' as 'a series of incidents moving continuously toward one end'.

There is no doubt about it, we do need organisation.
But Men of God will agree with me that we cannot
organise the Spirit of God!

Remember what the Lord Jesus said to Nicodemus,
'The wind bloweth where it listeth, and thou hearest
the sound thereof, but canst not tell whence it cometh,
and whither it goeth: so is every one that is born of
the Spirit.' We cannot lay down tram lines for the Holy
Spirit to move upon. The Holy Spirit moves according
to the principals of the written Word of God. And
sometimes we are surprised when He moves contrary
to what we think is the Word of God! He is not – He
is only moving 'contrary' to our interpretation of the
Word of God. He, the Holy Spirit, has done that to me
many times much to my surprise and if I am honest,
much to my annoyance!

So to me, there is a difference between an organisation and a movement. History has sometimes shown
movements 'have turned into an organisation or a
denomination' – and it can do good! But they eventually end up tied with all sorts of rules, regulations
and dogmas, where an infringement of the 'constitution' can nearly become a major crisis!

Their constitutions become like the Laws of the
Medes and Persians which cannot be changed or
altered! Movements first evangelise, then they
organise, then thy fossilise, finally, they apostatise!

I believe a constitution in its administration should
be structured in such a way that it can be bent, stretched, amended and made flexible for any emergency
which the Holy Spirit could create. The only time a
constitution should remain rigid should be in matters
regarding sin, conduct, example and testimony!

Speaking honestly, organisations remind me of

religious clubs made up of men with small minds and censorious spirits.

There are successful organisations, but they are only successful because they have men with big hearts, open minds, buckets of love and Holy Ghost enthusiasm!

That's how I see things! Maybe I'm all mixed up! Maybe I'm dreaming! So, if I'm dreaming, let me dream on, until the Holy Spirit in a series of incidents, moving continually towards one end – and that is to bring the United Kingdom to the feet of God's lovely sinless son.

If I may be allowed to say, there are leaders and churches who fulfil a mission – a destiny – who, if you like, are unique in their witness, vision and purpose. Who cannot be held down or shackled by all sorts of organisational dogmas and rules (which I do believe in spite of some who rebel against them, are important). But some places are 'different' and must be allowed to be 'different'. Personally, I think Whitewell is one of those places! The people of Whitewell have a strong leadership inside its community and are a disciplined people who respond to strong leadership. But they find it difficult to respond to leadership outside its community because of what they feel God has called them to do. Of course this is not to say that the Whitewell Church will not help any other church or denomination – far from it – Whitewell is always giving help and ministry, when invited to do so and does very willingly with no strings attached.

Some people, from time to time, raise their eyebrows at the generosity of the Whitewell Church – giving and looking for nothing in return. Some pastors at first couldn't believe it. It was too good to be true – but many have found it to be so.

Of course the argument is raised: but what if the support is wasted? What if the money is wasted? You need safeguards! Frankly, if fellowship and working

together are not cemented in love and trust, all the
'legal bindings' and 'safeguards' mean nothing!

Don't forget, the apostolic band had its Judas! The
Early Church had its Demas, its Diotrephes, its
Hymenaeus and its Philetus. I'm sorry to say, the
twentieth-century Church will have the same type of
deserters, usurpers and men who love to have the pre-
eminence. But that's the chance you must take in
God's work. II. Corinthians 11:24 – 33, that great
chapter which deals with Paul's sufferings, tells how
on five occasions he was whipped by the Jews (nearly
200 lashes on his back), three times he was beaten
with rods, once he was stoned, thrice he suffered ship-
wreck, a night and a day he was stranded in the deep.
Then he goes on to say: ' . . . in journeyings often, in
perils of waters, in perils of robbers, in perils by mine
own countrymen . . . in perils in the city, in perils in
the wilderness, in perils in the sea . . .' Then he says:
' . . . in perils among false brethren'! (I think this was
the hardest one Paul had to bear.) And the same thing
that happened in the first century Church still
happens in the twentieth-century Church! There will
always be false brethren, until Jesus comes.

Everything we do must be done by trust, by faith,
by love – that's real fellowship! It is sad that we cannot
be like our blessed Lord, of whom it is recorded in
John 2:24: 'But Jesus did not commit Himself (or trust
Himself) unto them, because He knew all men, and
needed not that any should testify of man, for He knew
what was in man.'

Sometimes the Holy Spirit in His mercy would check
us regarding certain individuals. But alas! that is not
too often, so we have got to work together, trusting
and loving each other, knowing that one day as God's
servants and a local church, our work will be tried
and examined by fire at the Bema Seat! And Paul in
no uncertain way lets us know in I Corinthians 3:13:
'Every man's work shall be made manifest: for the day

shall declare it, because it shall be revealed by fire; and the fire shall try every man's work of what sort it is.' That's going to be some day for every servant of God and for those who have built their own empires instead of His kingdom! I would like to mention a personal honour that took place on 19th July 1986. To my surprise and amazement I received a communication from the California Graduate School of Theology – a faculty with very high standards in academic and Christian training – that they wished to bestow upon me an honorary Doctorate of Divinity for my services rendered to the Christian Church in evangelism, pastoral counselling and teaching.

My good friend Dr Basil Jackson Ph.D., one of the world's leading psychiatrists, together with Professor Robert McBirnie, came with cap and gown and before a packed congregation at Whitewell placed the hood upon me!

But let me say, I only accepted the honour on behalf of the Whitewell people who have constantly loved me, backed me and supported me. Before God, I am nothing without them – they have shown me great encouragement and tolerance as they have worked with me all over this country.

I know sometimes they don't understand me but they believe in me as the prophet Jehosaphat told the people of Judah: 'Believe in the Lord your God. Believe His prophets and ye shall prosper.' Whitewell has prospered over the years for God has rewarded them for their faithfulness and their work of love. So what was bestowed upon me on 19th July, 1986, was really an honour to the Whitewell people and I take advantage of this book to say to them: 'I love you, and long may you reign in this land, bringing the presence of Christ to the people!'

16

My land and my city

Since that April night in 1955 when as a seventeen-
year-old boy, I entered into the ministry and full-time
service for the Lord, the Master in His grace has taken
me to many different countries and given me the
honour of ministering to many nationalities.

I have had the privilege of preaching in various
parts of the British Isles, Spain, Holland, Belgium,
Germany, France, Romania, Bulgaria, Yugoslavia,
Austria, Canada, Israel, Columbia, Guatemala, El
Salvador, Panama, North Africa, Central Africa and
literally scores of times in the United States of
America.

But very often I have been asked: Do you not get
tired of staying in the one church for over thirty years?
Do you not get bored with the parochial political situation existing in Northern Ireland? Why not take
advantage of the many offers which have been made
to you to leave your church and your country and
minister where conditions are better and more
comfortable financially and economically?

My answer to such questions is found in one
sentence: I believe there is such a thing for a man's
life as the 'will of God'. Many people find it difficult to
know what the 'will of God' is for their lives, but
personally speaking, I know that for the past thirty
years the cream of my life, the best years of my life

had to be given to the Whitewell people, and it appears up to now that that is the way things are going to continue.

Of course there have been times when I felt a change would do me good and the Whitewell people good! But then, another 'wave of blessing' comes along which blots out all such feelings. However, I have made it absolutely clear that I will stay as long as the Whitewell people want me to stay and when I find the majority of them are tiring of me, it will then be time for me to seek the Lord and ask Him for another door of service. If that day ever comes, it will be a sad day for me – for I love these Whitewell people with all my heart. Pastoring and being in Whitewell is like a marriage – Whitewell is a church that is hard to get out of your system. Even when I am away on preaching tours or on holiday, my family get irritable and angry with me when I telephone the office or my pastors to find out what's going on – for they feel I should rest. But I can't help myself, Whitewell has been and is my life!

On occasions, I hear pastors saying (sighing with relief) how delighted they are to be asked to preach somewhere else or how much they are looking forward to getting away from their people. I can honestly say, I have never felt that way in my life regarding the church God has placed me in. I love these people. Maybe if the truth were known, the Whitewellers are glad to get rid of me for a few weeks! However, I never sense that.

Should there be pastors reading this book, let me tell you this. A long pastorate will do three things to you: it will make you read; it will make you study; it will drive you to your knees. For you will realise you have got to be fresh, you have got to bring fresh manna to these people every Lord's Day and at the mid-week Bible study.

I have generally found – but there are exceptions to

the rule – that the men who take up short pastorates
don't really build anything strong. I hope that no one
is offended, as this is just my personal opinion. I have
noticed often that men who travel and pastor from
church to church repeat old sermons and old corn. In
a sense it is an easy way of getting out of long,
laborious hours of study and preparation.

Upon reading the history of great men of God and
men whom God has used, I found most of them stayed
in the one place for twenty, thirty or forty years. It is
said that Spurgeon once remarked: 'The man who can
hold his congregation every Lord's Day for thirty
years, is a genius!' Well, I am certainly not a genius,
like the precious man of God that Spurgeon was in
his day, but I have experienced a certain amount of
fulfilment being in a long pastorate.

Regarding my country – Northern Ireland. I love
this little province with all of my heart. Since the
Anglo-Irish Agreement, which has disillusioned the
majority of my countrymen, I have turned down many
preaching engagements in Europe and the United
States, just to be in my own beloved Ulster – in case
I might be needed to help God's people!

There is no doubt about it, our little province is
going through a 'furnace of affliction'. But, at the same
time, I try to look at things sensibly – what country
in the world is not going through some kind of trouble
or other! Is this not surely a pointer that we are living
in the last of the last days and that our Lord's Second
Coming is soon going to burst upon us!

My feeling on Northern Ireland is this: the economic
situation is very serious and many people are finding
it hard. The 'brain drain', too, is affecting our province
as many up and coming intelligent young people are
away to various parts of the world to carve a career
for themselves.

Many fine preachers have left the province, sick of
the violence, the narrowness and the bigotry. Many of

them believe that we will be plunged in to an 'all Ireland' state where freedom of choice and freedom of worship will be taken from us.

Now to me personally, this is a challenge! It is not the time to run, it is the time to dig in. It is not the time to panic, it is the time to trust. To me, the challenge in Ulster is: to shine! A light is only effective in the darkness and I say if the Christian Church and the Christian leaders in Ulster have anything – then let's not run but 'shine'!

This is why I am staying in this province and working in this province, because I feel in my small way I have a contribution to make for the good of all its population, whether they be Protestant or Catholic. My contribution is the gospel, the only vehicle I can see that can unite the people of this province.

Don't forget Paul in Romans 1:16 described the gospel as 'the power of God'. This gospel, as the apostle Peter says, was 'preached . . . with the Holy Ghost sent down from heaven', making it tremendously powerful. This gospel took one hundred and twenty people in an upper room, and inside forty years penetrated the Greek world, the Roman world, the Barbarian world – until that generation knew of a person called Jesus of Nazareth who was the Son of God – God of very God manifested in the flesh.

This gospel is just the same today. We need men totally abandoned to the gospel who passionately believe in it, preaching it in the power (the Greek word is *dunamis*; our English word is 'dynamite') of the Holy Spirit.

The gospel right down through history has always had its casualties – men and women who have been put to death for preaching and standing for the gospel – because the gospel casts its ripples right across every walk of life and every aspect of man's living and conduct, physically, materially, politically and spiritually.

I feel with all my heart that before this little province of ours experiences a Heaven-sent, Holy Ghost revival, men of God who speak out with a clear, honest and prophetic voice will, some of them, pay the ultimate price – the price of their own lives. For they will consciously and unconsciously smite on conscience and pull away the masks that hide men from their true selves.

There are enough evil men on both sides of the political divide who have a vested interest in keeping this country's troubles constantly boiling. And when a Daniel or a Jeremiah or a John the Baptist comes along, rebuking their sin, exposing their hypocrisy, spoiling their game – they will take steps to silence that voice!

This is my prime reason for staying in the Whitewell Church and staying in my beloved Ulster.

17

The secret of Whitewell's success

During the past five years many pastors have telephoned me asking for an interview, putting to me the question: 'How and why has Whitewell become such a successful church?'

The word which makes me stumble here is the word 'success'. Personally I have an aversion to it, and yet the word 'success' is a Bible word. I am reminded that when the time came for Joshua to take up where Moses left off, God said to Joshua 'This book of the law shall not depart out of thy mouth; but thou shalt meditate therein day and night, that thou mayest observe to do according to all that is written therein: for then thou shalt make thy way prosperous, and then thou shalt have good success.' (Josh. 1:8.)

So the word 'success' is a Bible word – a word which God has used Himself. But quite honestly, I don't really know if Whitewell is a successful church.

I have found there is no magic formula for success and blessing. Yet our Christian bookshops are full of books with titles like: *How to Become a Soul Winner, How to Pack Your Church, How to Increase Your Membership.* It seems if you can learn the formula and find the recipe then you have it made! But is it as simple as all that?

I remember some years ago, going to what was known as a 'Soul Winner's Conference'. There, I heard a man lecturing on how to bring a soul to the state of conversion! I felt constrained to go and have a word with him to find out what experience he had personally in 'soul winning'. He had practically none! Yet here he was lecturing, giving what he thought were the essential points in 'soul winning'. His success – if you want to call it that – was very meagre indeed.

Lately, I have been amazed at the rapid increase in seminars and the fact that hundreds of pastors attend them. Personally, I have attended one or two and the only thing I have enjoyed is the fellowship. In other respects, I have gained little from the experience. I remember an observer remarking to me some years ago: 'Show me your church and I'll show you how strong your leader is!' The man obviously believed in a strong, spiritual leadership. I believe the secret of any church's success and blessing is reflected in the leadership. And if that leadership is anointed leadership, Holy Ghost leadership, then it is going to motivate the membership and laity of the church. If the leader cannot motivate and inspire those under his charge, he and his church are not going to get anywhere.

The command the Lord Jesus gave to His disciples in Luke 24:49 is still valid and holds good for me. 'And, behold, I send the promise of my Father upon you: but tarry ye in the city of Jerusalem, until ye be endued with power from on high.' Some translations have the word 'endued' as 'clothed' with power from on high.

The Holy Spirit in John Mark's upper room was put on the 120 disciples like an overcoat – and they became effective persuaders, leaders. Totally convinced that Jesus was alive, they in turn convinced others. They spoke with conviction, they spoke with power and they believed themselves and thrilled themselves with what they were saying.

Before I can convince someone, I must be convinced myself. Before I can motivate others, I must be motivated myself. Before I can strengthen, I myself must be strong. Before I can get others committed, I must be committed. And, before I can get others to give, I must also give myself to show those I am trying to convince and motivate that I'm not asking them to do something I am not prepared to do myself.

Furthermore, if the leader is 'wishy-washy' regarding sin, then the standard of righteousness in the church will be 'wishy-washy'.

If the leader is weak in prayer, so will the church be weak in its communication with God.

If the leader is too spineless to rebuke hypocrisy, so will his congregation be spineless in their daily living.

If the leader is lukewarm in his dedication to his divine Lord, so will the church of his charge be lukewarm in their dedication.

But if the leader is in love with Jesus Christ, it will show, it will glow, it will flow. It will cause a reaction in the hearts of the congregation.

We need a company of God-anointed, God-inspired, and God-loving leaders in this nation. When we get them – the sickness that plagues the United Kingdom will be healed.

Many years ago, an old man who heard me preach a number of times, gently took me aside and said in my ear: 'Son, always feel responsible, always feel that everything is depending on you and when things go wrong in the church – blame yourself!' He was a retired minister and someone had shared this with him in his younger day.

Now, that advice may not be totally perfect, but it makes a lot of sense. In fact, it is as good as any advice I have ever received and I have endeavoured to take it seriously all of my ministerial life.

A leader is a responsible man, he is responsible under God for the church's success or failure.

The mark of a poor leader is that he will be looking for scape goats and excuses to justify his lack of success.

Brother, say nothing! Secretly cry unto God – He knows your heart, He knows your motive – but never forget the old proverb: 'He who excuses himself, accuses himself'.

Aaron, the brother of Moses, was a leader and he showed during the crisis of the Golden Calf just how weak a leader he really was. Remember when the angry Moses came on the scene demanding to know from Aaron exactly what had happened, Aaron replied: ' . . . they said unto me, make us gods, which shall go before us: for as for this Moses, the man that brought us up out of the land of Egypt, we wot not what is become of him. And I said unto them, Whosoever hath any gold, let them break it off. So they gave it me: then I cast it into the fire, and there came out this calf.' (Exod. 32:23–24.)

It is hard to believe that this was a leader speaking – it was as if the whole matter had been a thing of merely natural evolution and not of deliberate manufacture!

But that is always the reaction and the characteristic of weak leadership. It is never his fault – it is always someone else's, or it 'just happened'!

Be strong – even be strong when you have failed! Take your medicine and if God has truly called you, you will find Him a most gracious, tender, understanding and forgiving Lord. But never put the blame of the 'lack of success' on someone else. Don't let yourself say: 'The reason that man is successful is because the place he is in is conducive to a move of God'. For wherever the Holy Ghost is – that place will become conducive to the movings of Almighty God.

Maybe these thoughts are not altogether perfect, but

this is what I have found in my own life and ministry. I am saying all this to try to answer the questions put to me concerning the secret of Whitewell's success.

What has happened in Whitewell has been team work. We have been partners, we have been workers together with God. But before that came about, someone had to be first of all convinced he had a vision and that he had a call from God. The proof of that was that the Holy Spirit in His grace gave him the ability to transfer that vision to others, thus convincing them. As one Ulsterman quaintly asked (only Ulster people could put it this way): 'Do you really believe in what you believe?'

What you really believe determines your conduct, your behaviour and your emphasis.

I know this may sound contradictory – but, nevertheless, it is true. There is such a thing as a 'dead faith', a faith that just talks and does nothing else. I'm afraid that's the story of many leaders and of many churches throughout the world today.

Real faith is active, real faith is alive, genuine faith is positive. As the writer to the Hebrews says in that great 'faith gallery' of chapter 11: 'Now faith is the substance of things hoped for, the evidence of things not seen.'

What does he mean? His words can be translated: 'We are convinced that we have what we do not see.' The Greek word for 'evidence' in Hebrews 11:1 can be translated 'demonstration', so the verse reads: 'Now faith is the substance of things hoped for, the demonstration of things not seen.' Or as James in his Epistle puts it: 'For as the body without the spirit is dead, so faith without works is dead' – being alone. (Jas. 2:26).

That's the secret of Holy Ghost leadership and, to me, the 'open secret' why the Whitewell Church has enjoyed a measure of blessing. When this living faith gets the hold of a leader and of his congregation – things happen!

But first, it must get hold of the leader. Do you remember the appalling incident recorded in Numbers 13, when God commanded Moses to send out twelve spies to search out the land of Caanan to observe its strength, its weakness and to study the people – then to bring back their report?

In verse 2, God said: 'I want a man out of each of the twelve tribes, every one a ruler or leader among them'.

Verse 3 says: 'And Moses by the commandment of the Lord sent them from the wilderness of Paran: all those men were heads of the children of Israel.'

They were away for forty days. When they came back they declared (verses 27–28, 31): 'We came into the land whither thou sentest us, and surely it floweth with milk and honey . . . nevertheless the people be strong that dwell in the land . . . We be not able to go up against the people; for they are stronger than we.' Only two leaders out of the twelve Moses sent were convinced they could possess the land – Joshua and Caleb. But the said thing is 2,500,000 people believed the word of the other ten leaders, and those ten leaders by their word and example put an entire nation out of the will of God for forty years.

They forgot the Red Sea, standing up in two heaps!

They forgot the manna faithfully sent down to them for forty years.

They forgot the pillar of cloud by day and the pillar of fire by night.

Their faith was a dead faith – without demonstration. Only Joshua and Caleb out of that generation possessed the land, because their faith was alive, active and real.

I remember years ago hearing someone say: 'You are what your believing is!' And as Solomon put it: 'As a man thinketh so is he.' Don't be afraid, trust God, He will not disappoint you.

Christian leader, reading this book, get alone with

God! Ask Him to anoint you, to clothe you with power from on high. Ask Him to give you the ability that comes from the Holy Spirit, to motivate and inspire your people, and you too will have your own special success story. So from one pastor to another, I wish you every success and blessing! Should any of you in your climb to God's full purpose for your life need a chat – contact me! Sometimes a talk with a fellow servant of God, who also is 'hungry for God', can help and encourage.

There were times in the midst of great blessing where I found myself lonely and I longed for some man to talk to who had been there before me, and who had gone much further than I had gone. If I had found a brother like that, it would have proved a great blessing – a great boon to me. But I had to learn and advance by trial and by error. Even a fellow servant of God to pray with would have helped. But it seemed in those days as it still seems today that many pastors are nervous men, insecure men, frightened of losing their sheep. And so they are prone to stay exclusively in their own patch. They must be very lonely too, and my heart goes out to them. But God saw my heart and in the end gave me a staff, marvellously gifted, who at the same time knew their place, knew their ability, acknowledging their inabilities. These people are not only my staff, they are my friends. I hope these thoughs will inspire some man to lay hold on God and not let Him go until He blesses him!

In the boxing world, they say 'a hungry fighter' is not only a hard fighter – he's a climbing fighter! You see, he is hungry for success, and that of course is a lesson to the fighter who has already made it to the top. It's one thing getting to the top, but it's another thing to stay there.

Many times we have witnessed great fighters who have reached the zenith of their strength and success, only to become soft and indolent because of prosperity,

high living, high society and with the wrong people
around them. Then when this young, hungry fighter
comes along contending for his crown and place the
successful fighter has a long struggle to become fit
again, before he fights his crucial battle with the
hungry fighter who is ready to take his crown. The
words of the Lord Jesus to the angel or the minister of
the church at Philadelphia are very apt here: 'Behold, I
come quickly: hold that fast which thou hast, that no
man take thy crown.' (Rev. 3:11.)

What is really wrong?

Maybe psychologically as well as spiritually the
successful fighter has thought he 'has it made'. That
thought is his defect. That thought is the chink in his
armour. That thought is the actual weakness of his
success.

Never think you 'have it made'! Never let it cross
your mind that there are no more mountains to climb,
no more battles to be fought.

Paul cried to the Corinthians, 'Let him that standeth
take heed lest he fall.' And again, 'When I am weak,
then I am strong.'

Paul was always a 'hungry fighter'!

What I am trying to say is, when you lose your
hunger, you lose your strength. When you lose your
hunger, you lose your dedication. And, strange as this
may sound, when you lose your hunger, you lose your
zest.

There is a story which Halliday Sutherland tells of
how he felt when he first qualified as a doctor. When
on the street or in company, if there came the call: 'Is
there a doctor here?' he thrilled at it, proud and eager
to step forward to help. But as the years passed, a
request like that became a nuisance – the thrill was
gone, the hunger was gone. He had made it!

James McConnell has constantly to remind himself
who he is, what he is: a sinner saved by sovereign and
amazing grace and a servant of the Lord Jesus Christ.

My hunger must be for Him. My hunger must be for His purposes and His kingdom. If I lose that and cease to be hungry, then I will lose my edge, my sharpness and my power.

I would remind all hungry, climbing servants of God aiming for the top: high places are slippery places and it takes a steady hand to carry a full cup.

Keep your head. Keep your feet. Keep your heart humble before your Lord.

18

The tools of the trade

At this point I would like to give a little word of advice and comfort to those men who desire with all their heart to have a 'move of God' in their church.

There is one particular factor I have observed, during this past twenty-five years, in the Christian Church. The standard and skill of preaching has somewhat diminished. It seems that the Church of the seventies and eighties suffers from a lack of 'pulpit giants'. I know that preaching is not everything, but God has ordained that the gospel of His Son be communicated in this way – by men preaching in the power and demonstration of the Holy Spirit.

There is a current attitude that preaching is not important, and that God has many more methods of reaching people and attracting people to His house than this. In fact, one man told me with great enthusiasm that when this revival comes, preaching will be put in the shade! That sort of talk and reasoning is nonsense, for right from the beginning of the history of revivals (the out-pouring of the Holy Ghost in the Book of Acts) there was tremendous preaching by the apostles. In fact, Dr Luke, who wrote the Book of Acts, says in chapter 4:33: 'And with great power gave the apostles witness of the resurrection of the Lord Jesus: and great grace was upon them all.' The New Testament revival and the periodic revivals that followed from the first century until the twentieth century were always characterised by men preaching and communicating the word.

In fact, there are four things which are underlined over and over again in the Book of Acts. They are the Word, the Spirit, the Name and the Way. We are not really hearing these things any longer.

Today, in many churches, the emphasis has somewhat altered. We have music and ministers of music. We have choirs and song leaders. We have 'groups' who go around the churches singing professionally.

Lately, during the past ten years, we have had an emphasis on praise and worship. Many churches have entered into this aspect of Christian service with great gusto, saying that God is restoring again His house. In fact, I have visited many such churches with this emphasis – but found that the preaching of the word and the reading of the word was only incidental and not central.

In fact, there was very little time left for preaching, and if there were so-called preaching, it was painfully inadequate – revealing its lack of preparation and taken at random from some text of Scripture. One observer has said: 'The curse of the hour is sermonettes preached by preacherettes to christianettes!'

I am not saying that every church in this nation has gone away from the emphasis on preaching – but many churches have! I do believe there is a place in the church for all the things we have mentioned such as music, choirs and groups. In fact, if you come to Whitewell on a Sunday night, you will see and hear some of the finest Christian music in Britain.

But, speaking reverently and kindly, they are only preliminaries and helps. After these things there follows a Bible reading and an hour's preaching of the word. The average service in Whitewell lasts two hours.

So the people know that when they come to

Whitewell, they will listen at least an hour to the word of God. The word is important! The word is essential! Without the word, there is no life, as Paul puts it so brilliantly in Romans 10:14: 'How then shall they call on him in whom they have not believed? and how shall they believe in him of whom they have not heard? and how shall they hear without a preacher? And how shall they preach, except they be sent? So then faith cometh by hearing, and hearing by the word of God.'

Preaching is an art. Soul-winning is an art. Building up the people of God is an art. Fellow pastors, this is what God has called us to!

I like what the apostles told the multitude in the sixth chapter of the Book of Acts. Remember how the widows had been neglected in the daily ministration and this caused dissension in the church. So the apostles called that great massive congregation together and told them to seek out seven men full of faith and of the Holy Ghost to look after their business. However, notice what the apostles said: 'But we will give ourselves to the Word of God and prayer.'

This is the task of all pastors. True, the church you pastor demands many things of you; but if that church demands the time you wait upon God in prayer and the preparation of your heart in the study and the exposition of the word – that church is showing you that you are redundant as a leader; and that church is not going to be guided by the Holy Spirit, nor is God going to bless it, nor its pastor. 'We will give ourselves to the Word of God and to prayer' should be the motto of every servant of God.

I am convinced people still like good preaching. Every preacher, though he may be harassed by other things, should make his Sunday messages or sermons (whatever you want to call them) like masterpieces!

If a man can prepare his message carefully and preach that message under the power of the Holy Ghost, people will eventually come to hear him.

That is what Paul said to Timothy in II Timothy 4:2 – 4. 'Preach the word; be instant in season, out of season; reprove, rebuke, exhort with all longsuffering and doctrine. For the time will come when they will not endure sound doctrine; but after their own lusts shall they heap to themselves teachers, having itching ears; and they shall turn away their ears from the truth, and shall be turned unto fables.'

That time has come!

When fellow pastors and ministers come to my office to visit me (for a chat and a cup of tea) the conversation eventually swings to 'What did you preach on last Sunday?' 'Where did you get your thoughts?' 'How can you keep fresh and bring fresh meat to the people?' In answering their question, I usually ask them a question in return: 'What are you reading? What sort of library have you?' And many times, I have been astounded to hear of the scanty reading material some of these dear men have!

They look at me in amazement when I tell them of what I have read and of whom I have read – and of books I am searching for.

The servant of God is many things to his congregation. But to God, he is a student. Even in his old age he should still be a student. God's Book – his written word – should never be out of his hand. Those who write positively and believe positively about His word – their writings and books should be read and studied. That was the advice the apostle Paul gave to young Timothy in II Timothy 2:15. 'Study to shew thyself approved unto God, a workman that needeth not to be ashamed, rightly dividing the word of truth.' And again in II Timothy 3:15: ' . . . and that from a child thou hast known the holy scriptures, which are able to make thee wise unto salvation through faith which is in Christ Jesus'. He continues: 'All scripture is given by inspiration of God, and is profitable for doctrine, for reproof, for correction, for instruction in righteousness: that the man of God may be perfect, thoroughly furnished unto all good works.'

And again he said to Timothy in I Timothy 4:13: 'Give attendance to reading.' Even he himself, when he knew the time of his departure was at hand, the time when he would lay down his life for the Lord Jesus, said to Timothy in II Timothy 4:13: 'The cloak that I left at Troas with Carpus, when thou comest, bring with thee, and the books, but especially the parchments.' Paul was always a student!

I'll never forget what I heard as a young man, said by a great preacher to another young man whom I had led to Christ. They were in a Bible book shop and pointing to rows and shelves of commentaries he said: 'These books are representative of those men's life's work, they did this for you, take their life's work and consume it until it becomes part of you. Then you yourself will mature, you will get your own personal anointing from God.'

I never forgot that man's advice, and I took it, for I realised more and more the truth of what the Lord Jesus said about the Holy Spirit's coming to the Church. He said in John 14:26: 'But the Comforter, which is the Holy Ghost, whom the Father will send in my name, he shall teach you all things, and bring all things to your remembrance, whatsoever I have said unto you.'

For you to remember something, one of three things will have happened to you. Either, first, you'll have seen it; or, second, you'll have heard it; or, third, you'll have read it.'

The Lord Jesus said that the power of the Holy Spirit would come upon us and quicken our minds and cause us to remember and use those things He would want us to say.

God has a mighty anointing. But He needs someone or something to anoint! Get into your closet or study every day, read His word, pull down the helps and aids that sit on your shelves. Learn to break up your texts and find their meaning, then bring them prepared and fresh to your people. They will come back for more! There is nothing like fresh bread!

Some 'religious circus' and big time operator may come to your town. Don't worry – that guy is preaching an old sermon he has used a hundred times before!

Just keep praying, studying and preparing. Remember you are doing it to be approved of your Master and He has delightful rewards for you. He will bless His word and bless His people.

Some may read this and say: 'The Psalmist said: Open your mouth and I will fill it.' But before you open your mouth, first of all your heart has got to be filled. The Lord Jesus put it brilliantly when He said: 'Out of the abundance of the heart, the mouth speaketh.' There are some men who get up without preparation and talk – they call it 'inspiration'!

That could not be further from the truth! God will not anoint a man who has not gone into His presence, and prepared his heart and mind to go to the people.

You've heard of the fellow who said: 'I can preach for an hour and think nothing of it.' The reply was: 'And neither does your congregation!'

I am saying all this to encourage you to go privately into the presence of the Lord and study. If you do, He will bless you. He will bless your people and in the words of David, 'He will satisfy His people with bread'.

If you constantly do this, your people will learn to love and respect you as a man of the Word. You see, there are two types of men coming into our pulpits to-day: the man who wants to say something; and the man who has something to say! Which man are you?

BOOKS TO READ

Young students constantly ask what books have helped me and what books I use often.

There are books you will read once – those books are like 'passing ships in the night'. But there are others which (like the Elder Brother) are 'ever with you', because they stir your thinking; even if you don't always agree with the writer, he will provoke you and cause you to react in your thinking.

Matthew Henry's *Commentary* is the prince of them all! Spurgeon told his students to sell their beds and buy Henry! If you read some of Spurgeon's sermons from the 'New Park Street pulpit', you will find Matthew Henry's scaffolding – but Spurgeon brilliantly pads in the upholstery! To me it is sad to listen to preachers who have never read Matthew Henry.

Then, there is Spurgeon's *Treasury of the Bible*, and his *Treasury of David*, which is his special exposition of the Psalms. His *Devotional Commentary* on Matthew's Gospel is beautiful. These books have been meat and drink to me!

Then there is the controversial Joseph Parker, the London City Temple genius. His *People's Bible* is a wealth of information to servants of God. What must London have been like when Parker and Spurgeon were in it at the same time? Thousands came to hear these men that loved to pray, study, read and preach.

Then there is my old favourite. Everybody is not keen on him, but he will make you examine yourself and look into your heart – Alexander Whyte of Free St Georges, Edinburgh. In particular, his two volumes on Bible characters of the Old and New Testament are brilliant and full of sanctified imagination.

After Whyte in my life, comes Henry Jowett. This man makes me study. His book, *Passion for Souls*, will make you wonder why you are in the ministry.

Then there is G. H. Morrison who once served as Whyte's assistant. His sermon outlines are tremendous, particularly *Footsteps of the Flock*. To the probable horror of many preachers, I am also going to mention Professor Barclay's commentaries on the New

Testament. While in no way do I agree with his theology, his background on texts, customs and cultures, and his treatment of Greek words are outstanding. I know hundreds of sincere evangelical men who, while they don't agree with him, read him!

Once a year, I try to read *Spurgeon's Lectures to Young Students*. I don't think there's a 'Ministerial Book' to touch it – even those (since Spurgeon's death) who have written books on 'The Christian Ministry' – still the Metropolitan Tabernacle Man has the edge on them all! Spurgeon's Lectures drive me to my knees and make me examine myself.

Also every year, I endeavour to read *Foxe's Book of Martyrs*. Why? Because it reminds me of the price many Men of God paid for my religious freedom, that we still have an 'Open Bible' in Britain today because they were so willing to lay down their lives in order that it would stay open! Some might say: 'Reading such a book every year, would it not make you prejudiced and militant for the Protestant faith?'

These martyrs weren't prejudiced – they died at the stake or in the rack, praying for their persecutors, like Stephen, that God would not allow their sin to be put to their charge.

Foxe's Book of Martyrs was written just like the Book of Deuteronomy for Servants of God to 'Remember'!

There are many more, but these are the main men that I cut my eye teeth on and who gave me the 'inside lining' of my spiritual constitution! When I began to mature and think for myself and obtained my own anointing from the Master – all this came together to help me, up to this moment in time, to make the Whitewell pulpit a blessing.

Young pastor! Discouraged servant of the Lord! Feel free to borrow and take these suggestions and use them. Remember what Solomon said: 'There is nothing new under the sun' – and these suggestions are as old as the hills. No one is original – the only thing original about us is original sin!

Let us learn from each other and I pray from the depths of my heart that God will take you and use you for His glory and give you 'a House of Bread' that will feed many!

19

The years ahead

Recently, during a BBC interview, this question was put to me: 'What of Whitewell in the future?' The questioner probed further: 'Would you not admit that the work in Whitewell is built around a man? What will happen to that work when the man grows feeble and God takes him home? Who is there to take up the gauntlet? What provision has been made for the future?' The answer to those questions is quite a difficult one, for the writer has seen, over the years, many a fine work which has been a glowing witness for the Master, year after year – only to lose its lustre and impact when the leader has gone!

After the death of Charles Haddon Spurgeon, the Metropolitan Tabernacle went through a series of phases for approximately ten years and never really recovered. To the glory of God, the Metropolitan Tabernacle still is in existence today. But, speaking kindly, it is only a pale shadow of the great house in its former years. But that has been the story of many great churches and of many great movements. When the leaders died, it seemed the 'charisma' died with them! Let us be honest: after the first century when leaders like Peter, James, John, Paul, Barnabas and Silas passed on, there were men to take their place. But sorry to say, they had not the same impact or the same 'Holy Ghost' anointing those men had. It could be argued that those men were special. They certainly were! But really it was not they who were special, it was the risen Lord who used them who was special!

The incident which is recorded in the Second Book of Kings, chapter 2, never fails to challenge me. After Elijah was translated home to heaven in a chariot of fire, his successor, Elisha (if he was to succeed and have the same 'impact' Elijah had had) needed no less than a 'double portion' of the Spirit of God which had rested upon Elijah.

But watch him in verses 13 and 14 after Elijah is taken away. The sacred writer says: '[Elisha] took up also the mantle of Elijah that fell from him, and went back, and stood by the bank of Jordan; and he took the mantle of Elijah that fell from him, and smote the waters, and said, Where is the Lord God of Elijah?' Elisha realised it was not Elijah who was special – it was the Lord God who had anointed him! The rest of the verse continues: ' . . . and when he also [that is Elisha] had smitten the waters, they parted hither and thither: and Elisha went over.'

Now notice the reaction from the 'spectators', the 'lookers on' (and there are always plenty of those!) in verse 15: 'And when the sons of the prophets which were to view at Jericho saw him, they said: The spirit of Elijah doth rest on Elisha. And they came to meet him, and bowed themselves to the ground before him.' Who were the sons of the prophets? The future clergy, the trainees of Elijah's Bible School!

It is the same old story, the same lesson to be learned for all generations in the future: the sons of the prophets were convinced Elisha was the man! What convinced them? They saw the spirit of a man who had gone into heaven rest upon a man who was walking on the earth.

Elijah and Elisha were certainly great exceptions, because Elisha's ministry continued for about fifty years, which meant that the same work was going on.

Elijah not only met the need of his generation, but he built a bridge in the form of Elisha for the next!

It was the same with Moses and Joshua. The opening verses of the first chapter of Joshua read like a great proclamation: 'Now after the death of Moses the servant of the Lord it came to pass, that the Lord spake unto Joshua the son of Nun, Moses' minister, saying, Moses my servant is dead; now therefore arise, go over this Jordan, thou, and all this people, unto the land which I do give to them, even to the children of Israel.' Moses' task was to bring them out. Joshua's task was to bring them in. But the sad thing after the death of Joshua was that it was many years before God's work entered into a settled, flowing, 'impact' stage. Instead, we have the period of the Judges, which someone has described as 'Israel's iron age'!

True, there were men anointed in the Book of Judges, but they lacked the charisma, the character and the knowledge of men like Moses and Joshua, Elijah and Elisha.

It is only when you go beyond the Book of Ruth, that you will read of a young boy raised up to be a mighty prophet – Samuel; and of another young boy, raised up to be a giant-killer and king – David. It is not until then that the work of God again is established – flowing with power. This is a pattern that time and time again repeats itself in the history of God's people. That's what concerns me about Whitewell – the place God has put me in. What of the future? What of the next generation?

I've thought about this most seriously. The only thing I and my staff can do is: with all our hearts, serve our generation in the will of God and try to the best of our ability to build bridges for the next generation – if God allows one! (For I believe His Son is coming soon.) I have found that some leaders feel insecure in their churches, especially if a man arises

in their midst with promise; they usually freeze him
or send him elsewhere!

Speaking honestly and reverently, I am constantly
looking for men with promise in Whitewell. If they
show themselves – they are taken by the hand and
encouraged to go on and study and above all to obtain
an anointing from God. For if they are not anointed,
they will only be wasting their time – thus the work
of God will eventually slow down to a crawling rate
or just grind to a halt. This has happened to many
great movements over and over again.

In Whitewell, we have a Bible School like other
organisations, where we try to train our young men
and women. But if the Holy Ghost doesn't lay upon
them and grip them – then all the training in the
world is not going to be of much use!

Bible Schools are essential – don't forget that the
prophet Elijah and the prophet Samuel founded the
'Schools of the Prophets'! But honestly, few ever
emerged from those schools with any impact. And it
is the same at times with Bible Schools – the students
come out like some comodity piece on a conveyor belt,
all looking the same, with ministerial voices, ministerial decorum, ministerial dress and ministerial attitudes. This is what I am afraid of in Whitewell! But
every week, I am looking for some man, some boy with
the vital magic, the vital extra, the vital charisma and
the vital difference!

What does this word 'vital' mean?

In short, 'the Holy Ghost resting upon him'.

Again, my staff and I have seriously discussed
building a bridge for the next generation. How do we
do it?

Well, once again, I take another great leader for my
example – David. Remember how he wanted to build
a house for God where His name would be glorified.
God gently told him that project was forbidden because
he had been a man of war and his hands had shed

blood. But the son who would come after him – Solomon – would be a man of peace. He would build the house for God.

Now, what was David's reaction because of this forbidden service – discontentment, apathy? No, he blessed the Lord who had established His throne, and then for many years set about gathering gold, silver and precious stones and the necessary materials Solomon would need to build the house.

Surely that's the least we can do as leaders for the future leaders – encourage them!

God has been gracious to place around me a group of young men, tremendously talented and hungry for the presence of the Lord. To me, they are tender plants in the house of the Lord.

I have met and talked with them for hours. We go out for meals together and week by week, month by month, I try, by God's grace, to get my vision and all that I know transferred over to them, praying that God by the mighty power of His Spirit will anoint them in their various capacities and use them mightily for His glory!

CHURCH EXTENSION

We hope by the time this book is printed that plans will be passed by the planning office for us to extend our church and build a great new youth centre beside it. The church will hold (comfortably) 2,200 persons. Some people say we should build it bigger. But I realise that I am not getting any younger and if I can fill that great house every week for the next fifteen years – I will accomplish something. In the meantime, those who are to take our place and stand in our place, will emerge to take on Whitewell's responsibilities under the call of God.

The rest of our young men will go out to pastor churches right through the United Kingdom and will

go overseas to do missionary and pioneer work. But
let me emphasise again, we are not out to establish a
denomination but a movement of the Spirit of God to
serve the remainder of this generation and the next
generation – if the Master tarries.

We have set up two financial outreach departments:
the first – Home Missionaries; the second – Foreign
Missionaries. Our plans are: if God opens a 'door of
opportunity' to send out a young man with his family
we will support him for two years. After that period
we will assess his work; if it is thought there is 'poten-
tial' we will further support him for another period of
time until he finds his feet.

Then we will let him get on with what he is doing
and start again with yet another young man, trusting
that those we have supported will remember how they
were helped and will in turn help others, starting a
chain reaction around the country of true Spirit-filled
churches and Spirit-anointed ministers in strategic
and needy places.

This is what I would like Whitewell to become in
the future, and I am planning to that end.

During the past two years, various people have come
and asked me what I think my ministry is in the Body
of Christ.

Really, I don't know, I love to pastor, I love to preach
the gospel, I love to teach, but I think my ministry is
found in I Corinthians 12:27–28 where Paul says:
'Now ye are the body of Christ, and members in
particular. And God hath set some in the church, first
apostles, secondarily prophets, thirdly teachers, after
that miracles, then gifts of healings, helps, govern-
ments, diversities of tongues.'

There is a little word tucked away at the bottom of
verse 28 and it reads, 'helps'. I feel now after my
fiftieth birthday my ministry is to be a 'help' and the
church I pastor is to be a 'help'.

This means, we are to be a giving people, not giving to ourselves, but always giving out to others.

I believe that what Jesus said in Luke 6:38 not only refers to individuals, but to churches as well. He said: 'Give, and it shall be given unto you; good measure, pressed down, and shaken together, and running over, shall men give into your bosom. For with the same measure that ye mete withal it shall be measured to you again.'

Solomon said in Proverbs 11:24–25: 'There is that scattereth, and yet increaseth; and there is that with-holdeth more than is meet, but it tendeth to poverty. The liberal soul shall be made fat: and he that watereth shall be watered also himself.'

I trust Whitewell will scatter in the right sense and in the right direction and increase all over this land and nation for the glory of God and out of that increase will rise up great men of God, great leaders – lovers of the Lord Jesus Christ to serve their generation in the will of God.

This is my vision of 'Whitewell' in the future!

Whitewell

A haven from the storms of life,
    A travellers' resting-place,
A place where hungry souls are fed,
    A Bethel of God's grace,
A shelter from the noon-day sun,
    The 'balm of Gilead',
The gate of heaven to my soul,
    A covering for my head.

A place of love in a world of hate,
    A pasture green and sweet,
Still waters where a soul can drink,
    A light to guide my feet,

A table that's prepared for me
  In the midst of all my foes,
  A loving, caring family,
    A comfort for my woes.

A pastor who will tend my needs,
  A brother who will care,
And sisters who will bind my wounds:
  A family who share.
A vanguard in the 'fight of faith'.
  How can a man e'er tell
Of all God's bounteous blessing in
  A house of love – Whitewell!

If you wish to receive *regular
information* about *new books*,
please send your name and address
to:—
London Bible Warehouse
Po Box 123
Basingstoke
Hants RG23 7NL

Name:...
Address: ....
....
....
....

I am especially interested in:—

Music/Theology/"Popular"
Paperbacks
Delete which do not apply